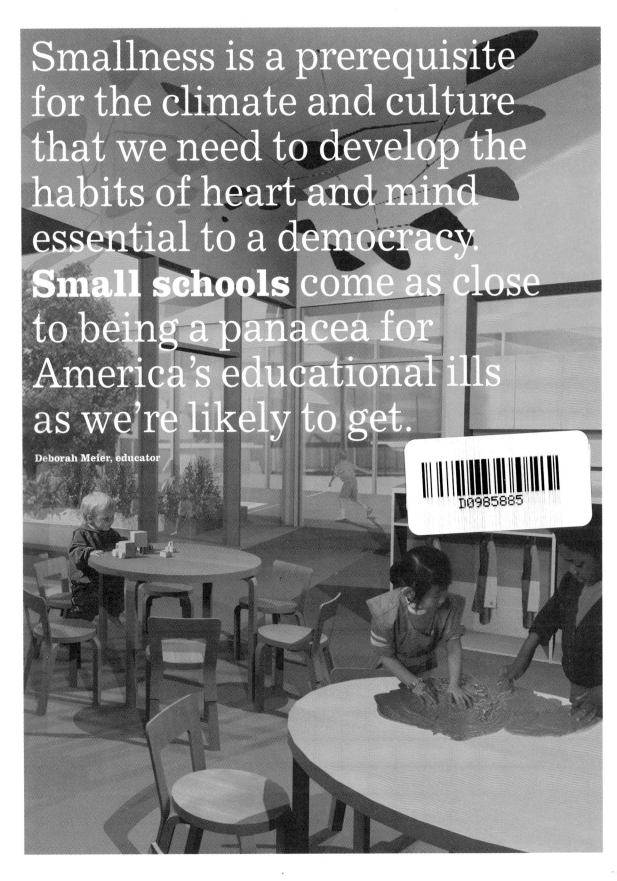

Smallness is a prerequisite for the climate and culture that we need to develop the habits of heart and mind essential to a democracy. **Small schools** come as close to being a panacea for America's educational ills as we're likely to get.

Deborah Meier, educator

Universal design is not an issue for the future, but a right for humanity long overdue. Universal design is not solely about ramps or wider doors; it's about all people being able to participate fully in our communities.

Marca Bristo, advocate

an inclined "main street" provides the primary circulation path through the school

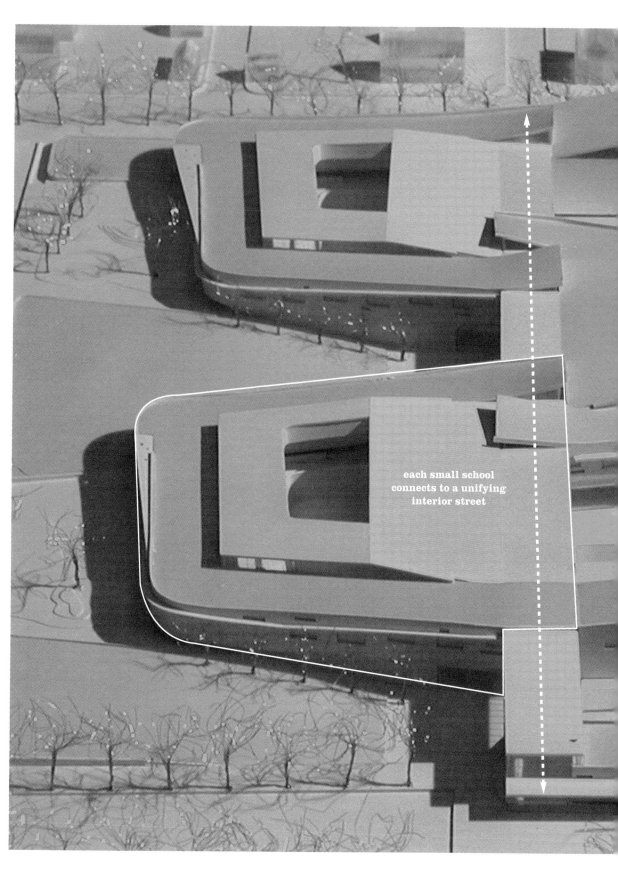

each small school
connects to a unifying
interior street

The physical world shapes our minds and influences the way we think and learn. Good design, therefore, should not be limited to those with the most resources. Every segment of society should benefit from thoughtful and **innovative** architecture.

Richard H. Driehaus, philanthropist and business leader

As the focus of neighborhood activities, an educational facility creates identity for the entire **community**. We think that identity should be as unique and diverse as the community it serves.

Carol Ross Barney, architect

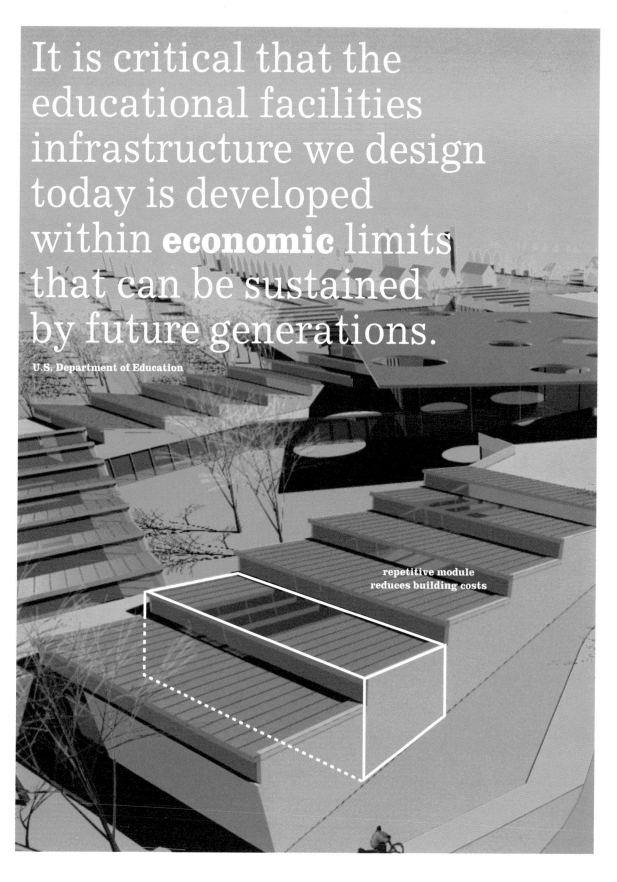

It is critical that the educational facilities infrastructure we design today is developed within **economic** limits that can be sustained by future generations.

U.S. Department of Education

repetitive module
reduces building costs

The Chicago Experience

First edition
Printed in Singapore

Published by Business and Professional People for the Public
Interest, 25 E. Washington, Suite 1515, Chicago, Illinois 60602
Tel: 312-641-5570; fax: 312-641-5454; www.bpichicago.org

Distributed by D.A.P./ Distributed Art Publishers, Inc.,
155 Sixth Avenue, 2nd Floor, New York, New York 10013
Tel: 212-627-1999; fax: 212-627-9484

Designed and typeset by studio blue, Chicago
www.studioblueinc.com

Edited by Robert V. Sharp
Printed and bound by Tien Wah Press, Singapore

Opening Sequence

The comment on small schools was taken from Deborah Meier,
"The Big Benefits of Smallness," *Educational Leadership* 54:1
(September 1996).

The comment on cost feasibility was taken from U. S.
Department of Education, *Schools as Centers of Community: A
Citizen's Guide For Planning and Design,* April 2000, pt. 2, p.10.

All other quotations in the opening sequence were made by
their respective authors in direct relation to this project or the
Chicago Public Schools Design Competition.

Photography Credits

All photographs featured in the essay "Chicago Public Schools
Design Competition," coauthored by Pamela H. Clarke, Jamie
Hendrickson, and Jeanne L. Nowaczewski, were taken by Jon
Randolph of Jon Randolph Photography.

Photographs featured in the essay "Chicago's Search for an
Architecture for Education" by Sharon Haar were provided by
The Art Institute of Chicago and the Chicago Historical Society.

Front cover: Koning Eizenberg Architecture
Back cover: Marble Fairbanks Architects

Business and Professional People for the Public Interest (BPI)
is a public interest law and policy center dedicated to equal justice
and to enhancing the quality and equity of life for all people
living in the Chicago region. BPI's staff of lawyers and policy spe-
cialists uses a variety of approaches, including litigation, research,
advocacy, community organizing, and collaboration. Currently,
BPI works to transform segregated public housing, revitalize economically disadvantaged communities, improve public education,
increase the supply of affordable housing, and promote sensible
metropolitan growth strategies.

Dear Friends of Public Education:

The Chicago Public Schools Design Competition, entitled "Big Shoulders, Small Schools," was a groundbreaking effort to add value to Chicago's aggressive school construction agenda and boost public awareness of the civic importance of innovative school architecture. I applaud the cosponsors, winning architects, and participating schools for their vision and dedication to creating school environments that exemplify our school system's academic push for excellence.

     This competition produced unique designs for two new Chicago public schools, and it continues to prompt serious discussion on public education for the future. Each school will serve populations integrated with students with disabilities, while ensuring that the learning environments be small, personal, and student-centered.

     Chicago continues to have great success in its efforts to create more small schools, largely through establishing "schools within schools" and developing smaller, more intimate learning environments for children. The recently announced Chicago High School Redesign Initiative, funded by the Bill and Melinda Gates Foundation and a dedicated group of local funders, has brought new support for this vision. The result will be the creation of effective small schools for Chicago's children and their communities.

     While I am proud of these accomplishments, I know that much remains to be done. Now, as the best and brightest architects work with educational experts to create cutting-edge schools, may the principles of universal design and small schools come to life and serve as models for all schools in the nation.

Sincerely,
Richard M. Daley
Mayor, City of Chicago

Foreword

Mark Robbins, Director of Design
National Endowment for the Arts

A familiar image of Chicago at the turn of the last century is depicted by Theodore Dreiser in the opening chapter of *Sister Carrie*: the city poised on the edge of rapid growth, bracing for a dramatic increase in population, a metropolis in the making. This scene came to mind recently on a flight into O'Hare Airport, as I looked down over acres of houses and industries, empty lots and construction cranes, City Beautiful parks revived and city streets replanted. Chicago one hundred years later is rebuilding its public institutions; it is once again, in Dreiser's terms, a "magnet."

The effort to remake a city by design was at the center of a program at the National Endowment for the Arts called "New Public Works." Begun in 2000 to fund national design competitions, this initiative has as its goal improvement in the quality of built work in the public realm. With the intention of starting conversations across the country about the potential of design, we saw competitions as a great way of giving form to innovative ideas and getting them beyond the drawing board. Designers would be given access to public projects and public institutions would benefit from the most advanced thinking about the designed environment.

In the first year alone ten competitions were funded for a range of projects that will yield new housing at the ABLA Homes for the Chicago Housing Authority, expanded facilities for the Children's Museum in Pittsburgh, and a new waterfront park in Seattle. In New York City, Dallas, and elsewhere, these projects will provide national models for new ways to think about our cities and the impact of design on public life. In this context, naturally, schools are an extremely important component. Students spend eight to ten hours a day in school buildings, which are probably second only to the home in terms of their developmental impact. I am reminded of my own education in boxy, red brick buildings with glazed concrete-block interiors from the 1950s and the crumbling Collegiate Gothic architecture of my high school. In spite of the generic space of my elementary school and the cracked and peeling walls of my later school, I received a solid and rich education. On some level it was the engagement of the students and teachers and the programming that made the experience so valuable. That high school, devoted to the performing and visual arts, has since received the new building that had been promised it when the school was founded as an experiment under New York Mayor LaGuardia in the late 1940s. The halls of this school are now broad enough that art students can sit and sketch figures visible inside the glass-enclosed dance studios. In many similar ways the school's physical structure has been tailored to the specifics of the program, and this enhances all the activities within.

We know that schools serve both children and their parents, and that the presence of a school can be a powerful component of neighborhood revitalization. In a city with a large and diverse immigrant population, for example, the school provides adult education in the evenings. School buildings also contain facilities such as auditoriums, gymnasiums, and health centers that can be shared with a community, creating a physical and symbolic center of activity. The Chicago Public Schools Design Competition sponsored by BPI and its partners has attracted national attention not only because it set out to make great schools but also because it was bold enough to insist on such issues as sustainability and universal design. A building should succeed on these terms and be an exceptional and challenging piece of architecture. The goal is to consider the way we design for all populations, often in unexpected and unfamiliar ways, to provide things of beauty that work and enhance our experience. I am grateful to all the sponsors for their support of this competition. Their contribution has been a profound statement of their investment not just in architecture or design, but in Chicago and its communities. The efforts of the BPI staff and the contributions of the architects whose work is depicted in this book should also be applauded. Their talent and hard work have raised the aspirations for public architecture and renewed a commitment to education. If children are to excel in a rapidly evolving society, they must be intellectually agile. This starts at the earliest age with curiosity in relation to the environments that we build. We all then look forward with great expectations as these buildings take shape in Chicago. They will teach us lessons that go to the very core of our lives as citizens.

Introduction

Cindy S. Moelis, Director, Education Initiative
Business and Professional People for the Public Interest

The competition entitled "Big Shoulders, Small Schools" demonstrated inspiring and realistic ways in which public school architecture can better facilitate student-centered learning and accessibility. The competition also modeled exciting, practical strategies for engaging local communities in the design process, and for partnering with them to make these new schools beacons for their neighborhoods. This book documents the work that resulted from the Chicago Public Schools Design Competition and explains the research and policies underlying the competition's criteria. The individuals and organizations included in our lists of Winning, Finalist, and Notable Architects and Educational Partners and Resources are available to anyone planning or building a school for children, their families, and their community.

This volume has three distinct parts. Book 1, "The Chicago Experience," written by the competition's organizers, describes the competition's process and explains how it allowed community members, educational experts, and architects to collaborate in the design of schools that will foster the education of students, support quality teaching, and increase community involvement. In a separate essay, Professor Sharon Haar chronicles the changing trends in public school architecture in Chicago.

Book 2, "New School Designs," provides a wealth of plans and ideas for schools designed for the twenty-first century. The competition's two winning designs and those of the finalists are extensively documented in drawings and renderings. Each of these architects has developed an expertise in community-based planning processes and understands the educational best practices so skillfully incorporated into their designs. Again, for anyone involved in the construction of new schools, these architects and their designs have much to offer.

Finally, Book 3, "Policies and Principles," explores policies that provided the impetus for the Chicago competition. Small schools advocate Susan Klonsky and public interest lawyer Alexander Polikoff discuss the advantages of smaller learning environments. City of Chicago Commissioner David K. Hanson and architect Jack Catlin and their colleagues explain the benefits of universal design to students, teachers, and the community. Thomas A. Forman and Rose Grayson explain the application of sustainable design to the creation of public schools. Professor Jeffery A. Lackney explores the importance of cost feasibility, a critical issue when building within a public budget. This section ends with a complete list of the winning, finalist, and notable architectural firms involved in the competition and a selected list of professional resources for the creation of new schools and the issues addressed in this book.

The structures in which we teach our children greatly affect how they learn. We hope that you will be inspired by the ideas embodied in these designs and apply them when creating schools in your community. In Chicago, we eagerly await the construction of the winning designs and the future benefits they will bring to their communities and children. Until the Chicago Board of Education fulfills its pledge to fund and build the winning designs by the year 2004, this book is the best way to share the expertise, energy, and creativity generated by the competition and design exhibition.

Chicago Public Schools Design Competition

Pamela H. Clarke, Associate Director
Leadership for Quality Education

Jamie Hendrickson, Competition Organizer
Business and Professional People for the Public Interest

Jeanne L. Nowaczewski, Director, Office of Small Schools
Chicago Public Schools

Chicago's public school system, like most urban school systems across the country, now faces the formidable challenge of rebuilding its aging schools, the majority of which were constructed prior to World War II. Chicago has blazed a trail in this effort since 1996, when it launched the nation's most ambitious school-construction program. After working at a breakneck pace for five years to build new schools and renovate old ones, Chicago afforded itself in 2000 an opportunity to take a step back and reflect upon how it could improve its chances of creating better, more responsive school designs. In this moment of reflection, the Chicago Public Schools Design Competition was conceived with the following goals:

1. To demonstrate cost-effective ways in which new school designs could accommodate the smaller learning communities that research has unequivocally shown to aid teaching and learning, while also incorporating state-of-the-art features that enhance accessibility and sustainability.

2. To model replicable strategies for facilitating involvement of the school community throughout the design process.

3. To generate a broad, citywide dialogue about the importance of innovative school design for all of Chicago.

When the competition concluded in summer of 2001, these goals were not only met, they were surpassed: once funding is secured, the Chicago Board of Education has pledged to build the two winning designs – one in the city's South Side community of Roseland and one in the Irving Park neighborhood on the North Side.

Innovative Partnerships

The Chicago Public Schools Design Competition also demonstrated how new partnerships can leverage the best possible results for the students and communities of Chicago. The seed for the competition was planted by teachers and principals who, inspired by research on the efficacy of small schools and by their colleagues' positive experiences with smaller, more student-centered learning environments, were themselves struggling to create such schools within inflexible large-school buildings that resisted their efforts. Frustrated, these educators asked, "If Chicago is gearing up to build dozens of schools, each with a capacity of 800 students, why not design these new facilities so that they can at least be capable of subdivision into three small schools?" Each school could choose whether to subdivide or not, but buildings constructed according to this principle would also make it easier for neighborhoods to utilize the facilities before and after school hours.

In response to these ideas, two Chicago-based advocates for small schools – Business and Professional People for the Public Interest (BPI) and Leadership for Quality Education (LQE) – formed the idea for a school-design competition to increase awareness of these issues and attract the best and brightest architects to propose solutions. BPI and LQE proposed the competition concept to the Chicago Public Schools (CPS), and CPS responded enthusiastically. The school system had, in fact, four existing primary-level school communities in mind – two on the South Side and two on the city's North Side – that badly needed new facilities and that could be combined. Both Davis Developmental Center on the South Side and Frederick Stock School on the North Side served student bodies of approximately 100 physically and cognitively disabled pre-kindergarten and kindergarten students. Davis was paired with Langston Hughes School, which served approximately 500 predominantly African-American pre-k to eighth-grade students and offered an award-winning Japanese language and culture program. Stock was paired to join with Inter-American Magnet School, a North Side school that provided 600 pre-k to eighth-grade students with a highly innovative Spanish dual-language immersion program.

If these mergers took place, approximately twenty percent of the students at each new school would be disabled. Thus, the buildings and classrooms would need to be fully accessible to people of all ability levels. While the inclusion of disabled students at this scale is uncommon and highly innovative, the trend in society is undeniably moving toward making public buildings fully accessible to all people. Excited to bring its extensive expertise in accessibility and universal design to the area of school design, the Mayor's Office for People with Disabilities, directed by Larry Gorski, joined as a sponsor of the competition. Sadly, Larry Gorski passed away in the fall of 2000, and the competition was dedicated to him in memory of the guiding role he played in its development.

In January 2000, The Richard H. Driehaus Foundation provided the funding needed to kick-start the competition. The Driehaus Foundation's gift ultimately leveraged broad support from other local and national sponsors, including the National Endowment for the Arts, which awarded the competition one of ten "New Public Works" grants given nationally. Critical support also came from the Reva and David Logan Foundation, Graham Foundation for Advanced Studies in the Fine Arts, Oppenheimer Family Foundation, Chicago Association of Realtors Education Foundation, Polk Bros. Foundation, and Chicago Architecture Foundation, and others who contributed valuable in-kind support.

The Competition's Structure and Criteria

During the spring of 2000, a steering committee – composed of school representatives, experts from the architecture community, and individuals from each of the sponsoring organizations – was assembled to ensure that the voices of all partners would be heard. The steering committee developed the criteria for the competition and a structure that its members thought would best enable it to achieve its goals. They designed a two-stage competition that would allow for extensive community input in the initial phase and generate maximum responsiveness from the architects in the second and final stage of submissions. The steering committee also decided that the competition would issue an open call for competitors, but also include invited participants, architects who would bring established reputations to the competition. The inclusion of architects from the open call would also ensure that this undertaking harnessed emerging talent and distinguished contributions by individuals or firms who may have been overlooked.

1 Architects visit Frederick Stock School.
2 Architects present their designs at a community forum.

3–4 Competition jurors review and deliberate.

As for criteria, the steering committee determined that the winning designs would best reflect the following features:

1. Sensitivity to small schools design: The designs should facilitate subdivision into two or more schools-within-schools to create intimate educational environments.

2. Sensitivity to universal design: The schools must be accessible, functional, and usable by people of any age, ability, or background, and must include features of green design and sustainable design.

3. Innovation: The designs should bring architectural creativity and imagination to educational spaces.

4. Sensitivity to neighborhood context: The designs should complement the ethnic, geographic, and social fabric of the schools' surrounding neighborhoods.

5. Feasibility: The schools must be buildable for approximately $200 per square foot. (At 106,000 square feet, the buildings would cost approximately $21 million, not including costs for land, utilities, remediation, and medical equipment.)

After a rigorous portfolio assessment and interview process, a special task force of the steering committee selected the competition's four invited architects from approximately thirty across the nation who were considered. The four firms had all earned national recognition for their innovative design of public buildings: Mack Scogin Merrill Elam Architects of Atlanta and Smith-Miller + Hawkinson Architects of New York for the South Side site, along with Koning Eizenberg Architecture of Santa Monica, California, and Ross Barney + Jankowski Architects of Chicago for the North Side site. The steering committee also retained the award-winning consulting team Design Competition Services, Inc. to assist in managing the competition process, coordinating outreach, and assembling a ten-member jury drawn from the architectural community, the four participating school communities, CPS, and the school reform community: William Ayers, University of Illinois at Chicago, College of Education; Lance Jay Brown, City College of the City University of New York, School of Architecture; Marissa Hopkins, Inter-American Magnet School; Ralph E. Johnson, Perkins & Will; M. David Lee, Stull & Lee, Incorporated; Giacomo Mancuso, Chicago Public Schools;

Linda Owens, Davis Developmental Center; Bridgette Shim, Shim Sutcliffe Architects; Richard G. Smith, Frederick Stock School; and Dennis Vail, Langston Hughes School. With everything in place, the competition was announced at an August 2000 press conference. Sixteen thousand promotional posters were mailed, inviting architects from across the nation to answer the open call for submissions and to compete alongside the four invited firms.

Competition Stage One: The Open Round

The competition's two-stage structure encouraged community participation and provided architects with sufficient time to incorporate community feedback and jurors' remarks into their final design submissions. The competition's sponsors developed several replicable mechanisms to help the four schools organize, offer guidance to the architects, and keep the communities informed about the competition. To start, each of the four school communities convened its own task force – teachers, principals, physical therapists, Local School Council members, and parents – to lead their schools through the competition. These task forces articulated their expectations for their new school building and initiated a running dialogue with the school community with which they were paired to discuss strategies for integrating their student populations and developing small schools. In addition to the task forces, a series of community forums, beginning in November 2000, was scheduled to facilitate collaboration between the school communities and the architects and to raise broader community awareness about the competition, its major tenets – small schools and universal design – and the civic importance of school architecture. These forums also created an opportunity for the school communities to meet the architects and for the architects to see the schools' students and the facilities they currently occupied (fig.1).

When the open call for submissions closed on December 15, 2000, 115 designs had been received from architects across the nation – 58 for the South Side site and 57 for the North Side site. The competition jury then convened for three intense days to select four finalist open-call designs to compete alongside the four invited architects in the competition's second stage. The open-call finalists were Borum, Daubmann, Hyde+Roddier of Ann Arbor, Michigan, and Marble Fairbanks Architects of New York for the South Side site, and Jack L. Gordon Architects and Lubrano Ciavarra Design, both of New York, for the North Side site. In the spirit of open competitions, these four finalists reflected a range of experience and backgrounds, and included fledgling firms, professors of architecture, and veteran architects.

Competition Stage Two: Refining the Designs through Community Involvement

The competition's second stage was arguably its most critical and undeniably its most intense period. For the eight finalist architects, it was an opportunity to receive feedback and incorporate this criticism into their final submissions. For the four school communities, these eight weeks provided their best chance to influence the final designs. At a second round of forums, beginning in January 2001, the finalist architects presented their first-stage submissions to the school communities, described how they addressed the competition criteria, and solicited responses from the school communities. At the second community forum – a day-long, citywide event held in February – representatives of the four school community task forces presented to the architects and a diverse audience their schools' official reactions to the architects' first-stage submissions. These presentations included broad conceptual reactions, as well as fine, detail-oriented feedback. In addition, representatives from the small schools, universal design, and green design communities responded to what they thought were the best aspects of the designs and noted where improvements could be made. These forums proved to be a fruitful and highly interactive series of community events (fig.2).

In March 2001, the architects presented their final submissions and scale models, and the jury selected the winners (figs. 3–4). On April 11, 2001, the winning designs were announced to a packed house at the Chicago Cultural Center. Paul Vallas, then CEO of the Chicago Public Schools, announced the two winning designs: Koning Eizenberg Architecture, an invited competitor on the North Side; and Marble Fairbanks Architects, a team that had answered the open call for submissions, on the South Side.

Lessons Learned from the Chicago Competition

Why should public entities embark on competitions, and how are such competitions best conducted? What was learned from the Chicago Public Schools Design Competition in terms of designing small schools, incorporating the principles of universal design and sustainable design, and including community participation? Herein, we summarize some notable achievements of the Chicago competition in the form of "lessons learned."

Design competitions bring a greater diversity of ideas to a public system and help solve specific, sometimes intractable issues. The Chicago competition was undertaken to solve three problems: to break the dependence upon prototypes; demonstrate that universal design was possible; and prove that large facilities can be successfully articulated as individual, autonomous small schools. The *first lesson* of the competition is that it is indeed possible to create well-designed, architecturally beautiful school buildings that incorporate key small school and universal design ideas, meet public school budgets, and include community participation.

The most dramatic engagement of the Chicago competition was the community forum at which leading spokespersons for people with disabilities critiqued each architect's design, and the architects had to listen, explain, and defend their work. The architects later commented that their designs were much improved by the detailed input of the school task forces and others who participated in the forums. *Lesson two* must surely be that inclusive community participation in public building design is not only possible (at a modest cost increment) but also important, because it affords key benefits: immediate value added and long-term political buy-in.

Lesson three can be drawn from the design of the competition: the competition's steering committee debated long and hard before embarking on a hybrid, two-stage competition, combining invited and open components, and prolonging design development over two stages. But the benefits far outweighed any additional costs. The presence of the four invited architects gave the competition sponsors a pool of talent to draw on for the first community discussions and other early planning activities, while the open call brought forth new ideas from a broad architectural spectrum and introduced the challenges facing inner city schools to a new audience.

The *fourth lesson* can be drawn from the use of two sites in the CPS competition. The sites chosen helped solve political issues of equitable treatment between the city's North and South sides, yet were not so many as to be financially insupportable, or to cause advocates to lose focus and splinter their support. The use of two sites also increased participation by architects and citizens, and ultimately demonstrated a wider diversity of available solutions than a single site would have generated.

The value of multiple partners in an effort as ambitious as the Chicago Public Schools Design Competition cannot be underestimated and must be recognized as *lesson five*. The involvement of small schools advocacy groups, the Mayor's Office for People with Disabilities, university departments of architecture, Hispanic advocacy groups, the philanthropic community, and others, contributed a diversity of ideas and goals to the competition that enriched its ultimate process and product. These various groups together articulated the vision of the competition, helped keep it on course, and helped it to avoid political missteps.

  Lesson six goes to the heart of this competition: small schools are affordable and they inspire easily understandable designs. How does a system implement more small schools when existing buildings are behemoths and when overcrowded communities cry out for schools big enough to accommodate all their children? This competition shows how, with many breathtaking designs that beautifully resolve these issues.

  Finally, *lesson seven* must be that we are only at the beginning of what we can know about universal design. Universal design is so new that its proponents have only begun to articulate its principles. In general, the Chicago competition pushed the competitors to design buildings that would be accessible to all without discriminating. But universal design always asks: is this as inclusive as it can be? The Chicago competition opened many minds to issues of access. Here, as elsewhere, the important lesson is to keep asking questions, to keep open the dialogue of what is needed and what is possible.

Sharing the Lessons from the Competition

The results of this competition and the lessons it can teach us about using architectural expertise to promote quality educational opportunites are beautifully conveyed by the drawings presented in Book 2. Each of the eight finalists addressed the competition's criteria differently and creatively, demonstrating the many ways that small-school design can be incorporated into new school construction, in buildings that are more fully accessible and more sustainable than ever before. The crucial policy issues pertaining to the competition's fundamental criteria constitute Book 3. The Chicago Public Schools Design Competition revealed the best of public-private partnerships. It demonstrated that we can have public schools that are innovative without sacrificing affordability. It illustrated the importance of broad partnerships and community involvement. If we attend to its results, Chicago and countless other cities can make important strides in educational quality and opportunity, while demonstrating passionate commitment to the children they serve.

Chicago's Search for an Architecture for Education

Sharon Haar, Associate Professor
School of Architecture, University of Illinois at Chicago

Schools are cultural and political artifacts. More than any city hall, museum, or symphony center – which are one-of-a-kind monuments – and more than any library or post office – all of whose many branches reference the main branch – our schools, like our housing, are part of the everyday life that constitutes the urban fabric. The complexities of style, program, site, economics, and culture come together in the design of school buildings and the design of education for the city's children. How then to assess the history of public school buildings with regard to future needs? Certainly, advances in educational practice have had an important effect on the school as an institutional artifact of urban culture. But this is all too often offset by the dangerous temptation of nostalgia, which induces us to believe that our greatest possible future lies in the re-creation of the past. In education, the tension between the need to transmit culture as we know it and to educate students who will be responsible for creating the culture we cannot yet know propels all progressive pedagogy. The development of Chicago as a city provides important clues to understanding this history. As I will demonstrate in this brief essay, aspects of Chicago's educational past offer a persuasive argument for ideas for its future, ideas that undergird the Chicago Public Schools Design Competition.

From Frontier Town to Urban Metropolis

Chicago's earliest schools can be traced back to the early nineteenth century, when, prior to the incorporation of the city in 1837, all schools, whether public or private, were marked by their transitory quality and the temporary status of their housing. In a twelve-foot-square log cabin built by Colonel Richard J. Hamilton in 1832 or 1833 as a stable, teacher John Watkins led one of Chicago's very first schools, with twelve students, eight of whom were of mixed Indian descent, an example of "broad access" to education at a time when Chicago was but a frontier trading outpost. Another early example, the Rumsey School, epitomizes our notion

1.18

of a school as a harbinger of urban settlement.[1] Two stories tall, suggesting that it housed both residential and educational spaces, this building sat squarely at the intersection of two plank roads, now the corner of Madison and Dearborn streets, the heart of Chicago's Loop (fig. 1). I raise these two examples because an understanding of educational building lies not only in the changing program of education but also in continuing changes in ideas about who should be schooled, where this schooling should occur, and for what reasons.

Chicago's first true public school building replaced the original Rumsey School in 1844. Later known as the Dearborn School, this facility had 864 pupils before 1850, reflecting the fact that by mid-century Chicago's population was becoming less transient.[2] Chicago remained a city of trade and immigration, with more than half its population foreign born. Calculations of the number of students enrolled and the number of faculty employed suggest a ratio of approximately 80 to 100 students per teacher.[3]

Pressures on the educational system in the second half of the nineteenth century were enormous. First, the end of the Civil War and the shift toward an industrial economy led city business leaders to push for vocational education.[4] By 1885 the average number of students per teacher had been lowered to between 60 and 70, but the very next year, 1886, the state legislature passed the first compulsory education law, which meant statistically that if all students who were legally required to attend school did so, there would only be enough seats for one-third of them. In the same decade kindergarten programs were added to the schools. The marked rise in the student population and the need to add school buildings rapidly drove the increasing modernization and sophistication of the buildings from a technological standpoint, a combination of the state's commitment to educational access and Chicago's leadership in design innovation. As a direct result of the devastation wrought by the Great Chicago Fire, the 1880s saw a growing concern for mechanical heating and ventilation and fireproofing in school buildings.[5] The LaSalle School was relatively typical of late-nineteenth-century school buildings: three-and-a-half stories, brick and boxy, increasingly hemmed in by urban development, and probably overcrowded (fig. 2). Its simple façades belied an already complex school program containing prototypical elements, and often built from standard plans and criteria.[6]

By 1900 the Chicago Board of Education had a school for teachers, along with 15 high schools and 234 elementary schools, altogether housing a student population of 255,861.[7] In a discussion of the role of the architect in the design of schools in large American cities,

1 Rumsey School, 1830s (now demolished)
2 LaSalle School, 1880s (now demolished)
3 George W. Tilton School, 1909, 223 N. Keeler Avenue

William Bryce Mundie, who had been the architect for the Chicago Board of Education for five years until 1904, offered the opinion that the design of school buildings should not be given out to architects in private practice: "The system is too large and detail management increasing fast."[8] Mundie's McKinley School and Crane Manual Training School demonstrate the scale and new programmatic aspects of the design of schools for the twentieth-century city, just as both reflect the product of large-scale design organizations and regulations. Despite their Neoclassical detailing, these schools are buildings of the industrial city. They are pragmatic buildings, with their monumentality deriving from their size and just enough decorative features and scalar elements to communicate their importance as public institutions. In 1903 the decision was made to enlarge school lot sizes to incorporate space for playgrounds.[9]

The Progressive City and Public School Architecture

The highlight of Chicago school architecture was the brief tenure of Dwight H. Perkins as architect of the Chicago Board of Education from 1905 until 1910. Approximately 40 new schools and additions were credited to Perkins and his office. Perkins was closely tied to both the Arts and Crafts movement and the progressive cultural and civic causes that were the hallmark of Chicago at the turn of the century. If today we tend to look askance at the monumentalism and institutionalism of educational facilities at that time, we must remember that the public school was developed as an institution of cosmopolitanism: a vehicle of cultural assimilation and the economic advancement of urban youth. Perkins was a contemporary of John Dewey, whose writings on education and establishment of the Laboratory School in Chicago form one part of what has been loosely termed "progressive education" in the United States. Dewey's thinking and that of his colleagues was tied to the conditions of the industrial city: how to educate urban citizens *within* the city in order to advance the conditions *of* the city. Many of the principles that underlay the Lab School are at play in the current small schools movement, incorporating the intimacy and student focus of private school education into public school education.

Perkins's work is notable for its variety of scale, technical innovation, and complexity of program.[10] Among his innovations were the use of the T-plan to maximize light and ventilation, east or west orientation for classrooms, the stacking of gymnasiums and auditoriums, the distribution of toilet facilities throughout the building, the modernization of the mechanical plant, and strategies for simplifying construction while incorporating fireproofing. Looking today, for example, at the first-floor plan of the Bernhard Moos School (figs. 4–5), one is struck by the order and functionality he brought to elementary school buildings, many of which had almost identical plans yet divergent building façades.[11] Perkins is particularly known for the organization and detailing he brought to the building envelope. Thus, in schools such as Lymon Trumbell and George W. Tilton (fig. 3), the brick is organized in horizontal bands while the overall façades are reorganized to group windows and piers into a vertical monumentality, used to great effect to mark the major entries of the buildings. Perkins's insistence on innovation and variations of architectural style for each of the buildings, even when they might have been of similar plan, indicates the extent to which the school building – an element of both the City Beautiful movement and the Progressive movement – was becoming a marker of urban cultural development.

In addition to efficiencies in classroom size and plan organization, Perkins was also involved with the provision of facilities for different constituencies of students. His designs for the original Albert G. Lane Technical High School and the Jesse Spalding School for Crippled Children exemplify these concepts.[12] The enormous Lane Tech was among the leading manual training schools of its time in the variety and sophistication of its classrooms and workshops and the manner in which they were organized into a city block.[13] The school was equally known during its time for its founding principle: "to furnish a good education for foremen and superintendents of manufacturing establishments…. It was established in what might be called a mechanics' neighborhood, if not a poor neighborhood."[14] This form of technical education was seen at its time to provide as important a service as college preparatory schools, a notion of segregated yet universal education tied directly to the socio-economic status of the neighborhood in which it was placed. That the Jesse Spalding School for Crippled Children was and is still seen as one of Perkins's significant school buildings is particularly important (figs. 6–7). An article on Perkins's school design in *Architectural Record* noted, "This building is less interesting for its architecture than for its solution of one of the most recent problems in popular and universal education."[15] The classrooms of this one-story building were organized around a large, shared playroom, providing an intimacy not available in larger elementary school buildings. Ironically, as the city's accommodations for students with disabilities grew, so did the buildings in which they were housed.[16]

Perkins's departure from the Chicago Board of Education did not bode well for the cause of innovation in school design. The next president of the school board, Alfred R.

4–5 Bernhard Moos School, 1907, 1711 N. California Avenue
6–7 Jesse Spalding School for Crippled Children, 1908 (now demolished)

Urion, accused Perkins of extravagance and opposed "the notion of designing schools as unique structures."[17] School design has often been on the losing side of the struggle between pragmatism and individualism.

The shifting relationship between the city and its region that marked post-World War II urban development, combined with the baby boom and the northern migration of African-American and Appalachian communities, created the next phase of school design development in Chicago. Outward migration of the middle-class white population, expansion of the existing African-American population, the demise of Chicago's great industrial base, and continued segregation led to great inequalities in urban schools. While the overall population of Chicago declined in the 1950s and 1960s, the school board created a quantity of new buildings and additions, typically one- and two-story functional brick architecture, located at the growing edges of the city. But there was also an increasing density of children on the South, West, and Near North sides, and some of the new buildings in these areas replaced the deteriorating schools of the nineteenth century, while others were built in association with new public housing projects.[18]

In 1963 *Architectural Forum* ran an article specifically focused on the problems of urban school buildings, including the fact that so few were being built.[19] The two Chicago schools covered in the article, the Anthony Overton Elementary School (Perkins & Will) and the James R. Doolittle School (Skidmore, Owings & Merrill), represented opposite architectural responses to public education and urban renewal, though both used modern building technologies. Overton consisted of functionally separated units, with independent classroom sections three-stories high with four classrooms per floor. Architect Lawrence Perkins thought Overton exhibited a connection to Crow Island, his firm's celebrated elementary school in suburban Winnetka, because it used corner windows, with all classrooms looking out to the landscape, just as the structurally similar, four-story Ludwig van Beethoven School from 1962 (fig.8).[20] By contrast, the Doolittle School took the form of an urban monastery, organized around a courtyard (fig. 9). What distinguished the two different typologies was their attitude toward the landscape, with Overton directed outward and Doolittle inward. Overton became a series of freestanding objects disconnected from its urban fabric, while Doolittle turned its blank, fortress-like walls to its neighborhood. Most importantly, each conveyed and enabled a different idea of community. The design of Overton was a prototype for new elementary school buildings associated with urban renewal housing projects.

One important, but rarely discussed, school building of the 1960s, designed by another leading school design firm, Caudill, Rowlett and Scott, was the James Weldon Johnson Elementary School, a fan-shaped building consisting of a ground floor of shared facilities topped by three classroom floors (figs. 10–11).[21] Each floor contained eight classrooms organized around a common space for team teaching. Johnson was a predecessor to later open-plan schools. Each classroom was autonomous but opened to the shared common space; each floor contained an independent community that encouraged student-teacher interaction.

Chicago public schools were not spared the civil unrest that characterized the 1960s. In fact, Chicago served as a focal point for the battle for integration of public schools in northern cities.[22] The 1970s were a time of discordant exercises in school architecture. In the mid-1970s a battle ensued between preservationists and the Board of Education over the proposed closure and teardown of twenty-five of the city's oldest school buildings, some "almost 100 years old and more than half … built before 1900."[23] The 1970s were also a period of the reemergence of the large urban high school, as exemplified by Roberto Clemente High School and Whitney M. Young Magnet High School (fig. 12). They were built of steel construction with glass and brick infill and consisted of a low building containing athletic facilities and a taller building containing classrooms and other school facilities. Clemente High School was notable in that the size of the school relative to its site brought about a nine-story classroom building connected by a second-story pedestrian bridge to the lower building. Although not as tall, Whitney Young, located along the then new Eisenhower Expressway, was similarly organized. Buildings of this period were designed on the model of the modern corporate office park rather than the civic buildings of earlier in the century. Their size addressed the need to accommodate large numbers of students in large technologically competent buildings during a period when it was not seen as a problem to tear down several city blocks for new construction. Their scale if not their style continued the tradition of buildings such as Lane Tech, where the positive, democratic impulse to provide education for all students created large, impersonal buildings.[24]

In 2001 there were 596 Chicago public schools educating 435,470 students, an approximate doubling of the school population of 1900. One hundred years has brought about a significant variation of school types: magnet schools, community academies, special schools,

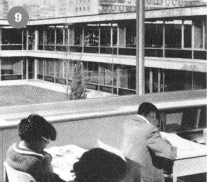

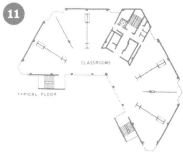

8 Ludwig van Beethoven School, 1962, 25 W. 47th Street
9 James R. Doolittle School, 1962, 535 E. 35th Street
10–11 James Weldon Johnson Elementary School, 1963, 1420 S. Albany Avenue
12 Whitney M. Young Magnet High School, 1975, 211 S. Laflin Street

middle schools, general/technical/academic preparatory high schools, vocational schools, charter schools, and alternative programs. This greater variety in school choice and increased parental involvement has also brought about a greater diversity in school buildings. The 1990s saw a reinstatement of Chicago's capital program for building new schools, including new college preparatory high schools and new smaller-scaled elementary schools. This period also saw the renovation of historic schools for new uses. Many of these larger and older school buildings, such as the Shakespeare School, have been subdivided for small schools following the principles outlined in the other essays in this volume. Other buildings have been renovated for new school programs, such as the John B. Drake School built in 1898 and decommissioned in the 1970s and recently converted into a transition center (by Bauer Latoza Studio). What has been important about the preservation and renovation of these older buildings is the effort to make them accommodate small-school practices and principles of universal education and the recognition that these older buildings remain significant for their integration into the built fabric of the city.

The Chicago Public Schools Design Competition is part of this return to the integration of schools within the larger urban civic program and the need to balance practical management with the best contemporary practice. In this context, small schools, universal education, concern for the landscape and the environment, and for students' tactile and intellectual experience bring together and go beyond the best thinking of the progressive schools of one hundred years ago. It also signals new processes of community interaction in the design of schools not present in the time of Perkins and Dewey. Combined with the realization that architecture and design are a significant force in the creation of the school environment and the school's part in making the larger city, these goals, as exemplified in the two winning designs, will serve as strong examples for urban education in the twenty-first century.

1 It is likely that this is the building that was used as the District 1 school, which employed Argill Z. Rumsey as its first teacher in 1840. The building was built as a house. See A. T. Andreas, *History of Chicago from the Earliest Period to the Present Time*, vol. 1 (1884; reprint New York: Arno Press, 1975). Chicago had a population in 1840 large enough to divide the city into four school districts.

2 Donna Rae Nelson, "School Architecture in Chicago during the Progressive Era: The Career of Dwight H. Perkins" (Ph.D. diss., Loyola University of Chicago, 1988), pp. 17–19.

3 In the nineteenth century small school buildings did not necessarily mean small classroom size. See Mary J. Herrick, *The Chicago Schools: A Social and Political History* (Beverly Hills, California: Sage Publications, Inc., 1971), p. 27.

4 Ibid., pp. 58 and 72.

5 John Howatt, "Notes on the First One Hundred Years of Chicago School History," 1940, p. 25. A copy of this document can be found in the Municipal Reference Collection of the Chicago Public Library.

6 Nelson (note 2), p. 21.

7 From statistics compiled by the Chicago Public Library, "Chicago in 1900 – A Millennium Bibliography" [http://www.chipublib.org/004chicago/1900/edu.html]. These numbers do not include the large quantity of students enrolled in various forms of parochial schools.

8 "The Architect and Chicago Schools: William Bryce Mundie," *Western Architect* 4 (July 1905), p. 8.

9 Howatt (note 5), p. 33.

10 Carl W. Condit, *The Chicago School of Architecture: A History of Commercial and Public Buildings in the Chicago Area, 1875–1925* (Chicago: University of Chicago Press, 1964), p. 201.

11 Dwight H. Perkins's work for the Chicago Board of Education is best summarized in Peter B. Wight, "Public School Architecture at Chicago: The Work of Dwight H. Perkins," *Architectural Record* 27 (June 1910), pp. 459–511. The article illustrates the development of and variations of this plan for different school buildings. Compare, for example, the Bernhard Moos, Friedrich Ludwig Jahn, and William Penn schools. The Board of Education's Annual Reports also illustrate many of his designs.

12 Wight (note 11).

13 The building was abandoned about thirty years later for its current, even larger, campus, known to have housed 8,000 students at a time.

14 Wight (note 11), p. 498. Children from poor neighborhoods, presumably, would not attend high school.

15 Ibid., pp. 507–10.

16 Various materials on the Spalding School in the 1930s and 1940s can be found in the Chicago Public Library, Neighborhood History Research Collection.

17 Carl Schurz High School. Preliminary Summary of Information, April 7, 1978, Commission on Chicago Historical and Architectural Landmarks. Space does not allow for a discussion of Schurz High School, another of Perkins's well-known schools. It is worth noting, however, that this school was originally designed for 1,000 students, but was expanded with two sizeable additions in less than fifteen years due to rapid population growth in the neighborhood that it served.

18 Unlike the Annual Reports of the turn of the century, which published plans and drawings of most new school buildings, the reports of 1958 and 1963 show maps of the city indicating where new building and renovation were taking place.

19 "Urban Schools," *Architectural Forum* 119 (November 1963), pp. 77–78.

20 Ibid., p. 89. The reference is to Crow Island School, a model for postwar suburban elementary schools by Perkins & Will and Eliel Saarinen. Perkins & Will, led by Lawrence Perkins, was the successor firm to Perkins, Fellows and Hamilton, led by Dwight H. Perkins. Perkins & Will remains a significant force in American school design.

21 "Decentralized Urban Elementary School for Team Teaching," *Architectural Record* 135 (September 1964), pp. 234–35.

22 Boycotts for integrated schools began in 1963 and grew into studies and legislation tied to the Civil Rights Act of 1964. For some discussion of these issues, see Adam Cohen and Elizabeth Taylor, *American Pharaoh: Mayor Richard J. Daley, His Battle for Chicago and the Nation* (New York: Little, Brown and Co., 2000).

23 Andy Shaw, "Weigh Closing Older Schools," *Chicago Sun-Times* (May 19, 1976).

24 "Mies' Office Tries Its Hand at Two Inner-City High Schools," *Inland Architect* (April 1973), pp. 20–22.

New School Designs

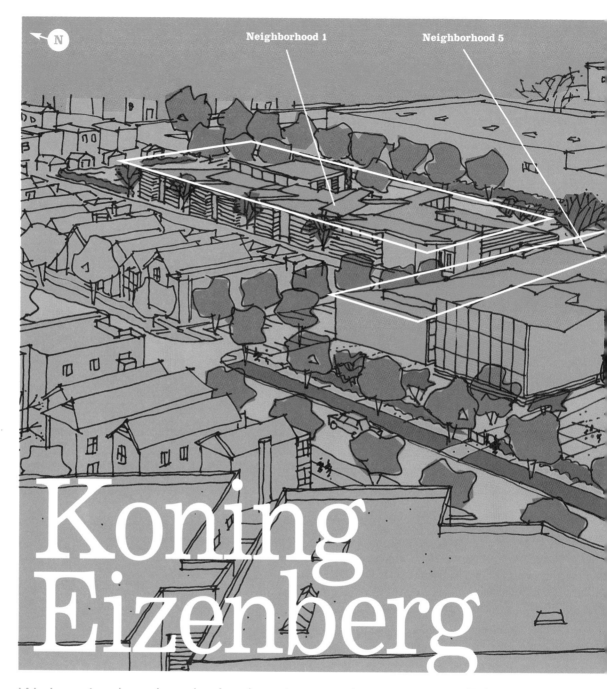

Neighborhood 1   Neighborhood 5

Koning Eizenberg

We imagined a relaxed school environment, supportive of the small school philosophy – a place where teachers, parents, and students could teach and learn most effectively. Our focus was each child's experience. Koning Eizenberg

2.2 Winner, North Side

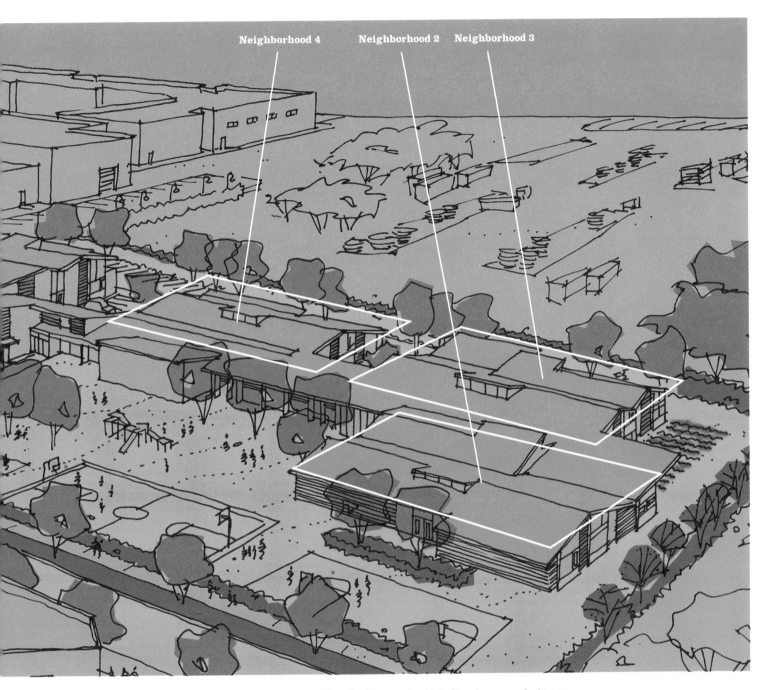

Neighborhood 4   Neighborhood 2   Neighborhood 3

This aerial view of the school, looking northeast, shows the elementary school wrapped around its large playground and, on the narrow, northern part of the site, the preschool building housing the pre-kindergarten and kindergarten programs.

The school is organized into five classroom clusters or "neighborhoods." Neighborhood 1 comprises the pre-kindergarten and kindergarten cluster of six classrooms. The elementary school constitutes neighborhoods 2 through 5, which are organized into groupings of six classrooms rather than the eight requested by the competition. This configuration provided sufficient flexibility to accommodate the school's current structure.

2.3 Koning Eizenberg

Neighborhood 5

grades 7 – 8

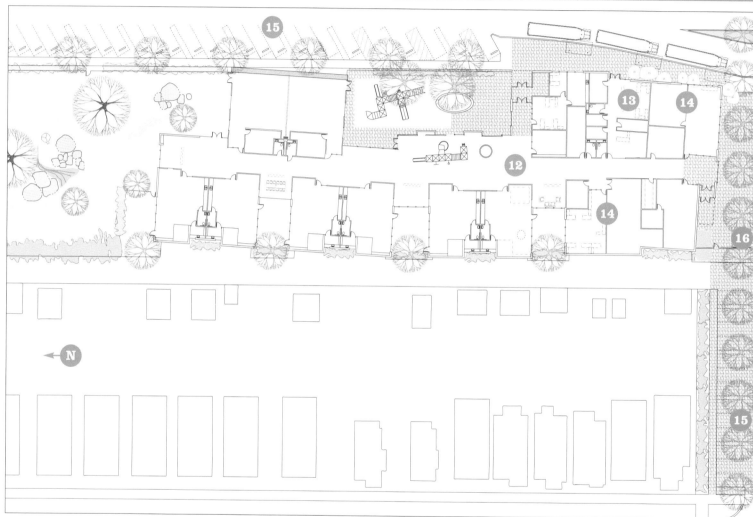

N

The oldest children (grades 7 and 8) could have their own small school — neighborhood 5 — on the second level, above the dining commons. It is reached by the ramp that circumscribes the library and links the library, art and science rooms, and the upstairs neighborhoods to the main level.

Closing the east-west street that divides the property enabled the creation of the Rambla, providing parking at its west end and a pedestrian plaza at its east. The Rambla safely links the preschool with the elementary school, and it provides a gathering place for special events and everyday activities like lunch in good weather. It is also the path to the bus at the beginning and end of each school day.

2.4 Winner, North Side

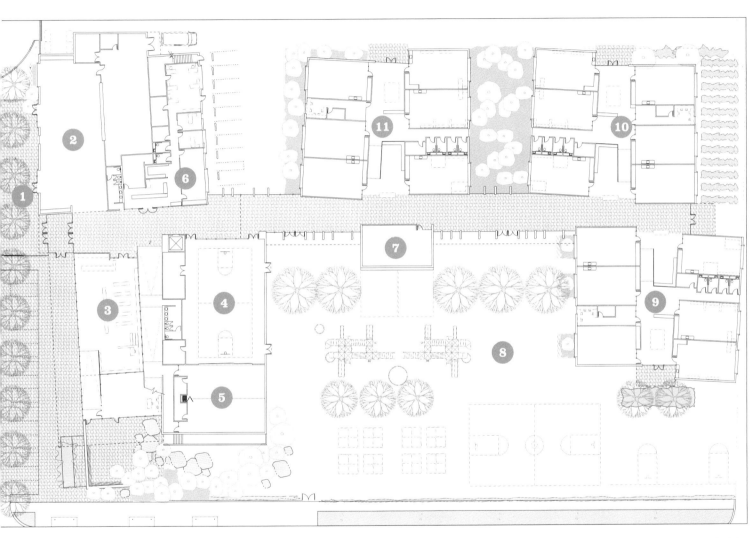

1 Entrance court-
yard
2 Dining commons
3 Library
4 Gymnasium
5 Multipurpose room
6 Administration
7 Music room

8 Playground
9 Neighborhood 2
(grades 1-6)
10 Neighborhood 3
(grades 1-6)
11 Neighborhood 4
(grades 1-6)

12 Neighborhood 1
(pre-k + kinder-
garten)
13 Health center
14 Therapy rooms
15 Parking lots
16 Rambla

The elementary school playground is a big backyard with
a variety of play options and experiences from places
to sit and chat, places to climb and explore, to traditional
climbing structures and large paved areas suitable for
competitive or group games. Trees provide shade throughout and define zones of use. A wild thicket provides a
visual backdrop between classrooms.

2.5 Koning Eizenberg

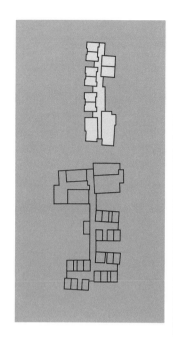

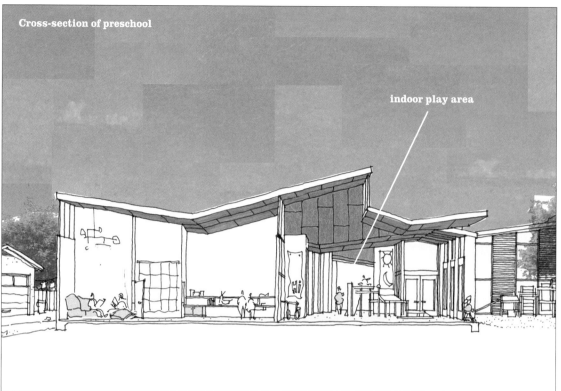

indoor play area

The preschool neighborhood includes the discovery center, the sensory stimulation center, and an indoor play area that allows children with restricted mobility to have a meaningful play experience all year round in spite of inclement weather. This area opens easily to the outside to expand the play area in good weather. Screened conference/viewing areas supplement the classrooms, allowing students, teachers, and therapists to meet casually. The facility is intended to accommodate all children and provide a welcoming environment for their families, with a dedicated parking area immediately adjacent.

2.6 Winner, North Side

The plywood panels that line the ceilings of the building above the entire stretch of its main "street" are varied in height and angle to create movement of light and shadow as well as mark programmed spaces.

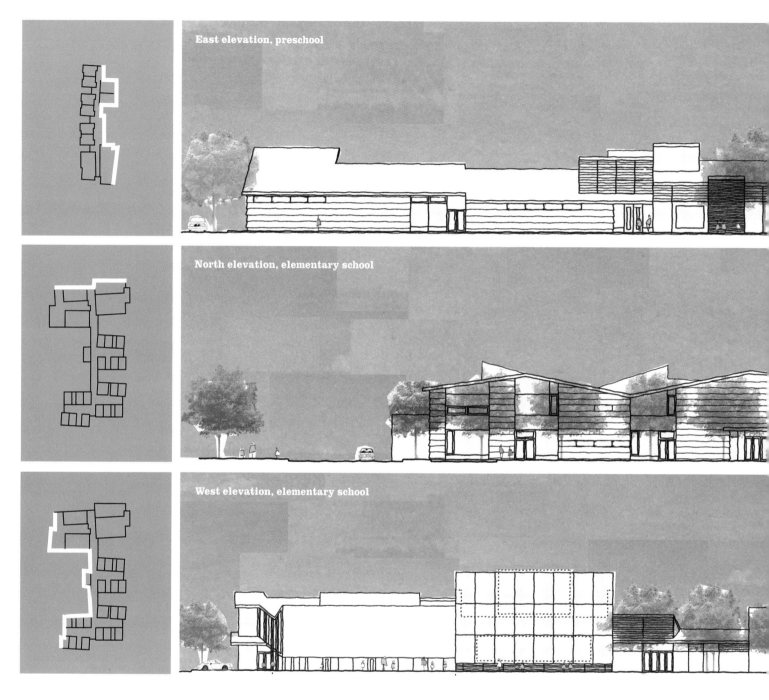

East elevation, preschool

North elevation, elementary school

West elevation, elementary school

2.8 Winner, North Side

The architects tried to maximize daylight for enhanced work performance, reduced energy use, and the sheer delight of being in the space. Thus, while a large amount of glass is used in the design, the east and west elevations show some strategies to reduce glass and therefore reduce the heat load by the use of fretted coatings without closing down the inside-outside connection. Classrooms are organized to face roughly north and south. South glazing will require passive exterior shading.

2.9 Koning Eizenberg

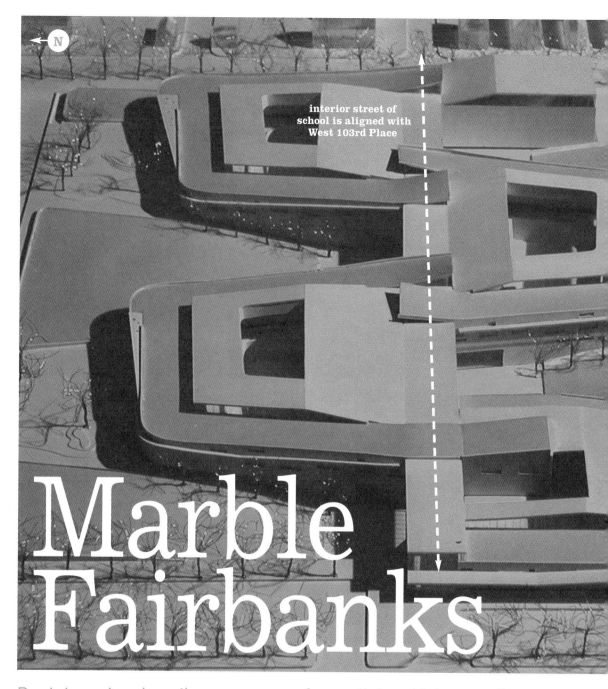

N

interior street of
school is aligned with
West 103rd Place

Marble
Fairbanks

Bootstrapping describes a process of growth in which a small amount
of energy triggers the evolution of a larger system. We believe a
school building can act as a bootstrap for the growth of communities
within a classroom, within the school itself, and within the neighborhood at large. Marble Fairbanks

2.10 Winner, South Side

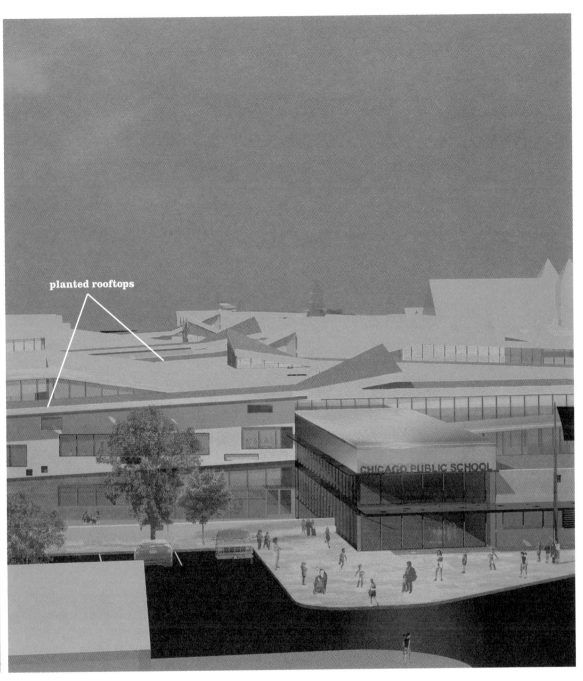

planted rooftops

The building is part of a continuous landscape, designed so that the building slopes up out of the landscape toward the center of the school, while the grassy play areas slope toward the interior street on the main level.

Continuity with the landscape is reinforced through the use of grass on the classroom roofs. Community involvement in the school is increased through the creation of a community garden along 103rd Street, the neighborhood's principal thoroughfare. This garden, which will include individual plots, paths, benches, and public art projects, invites the community into the school site. Community use also extends to the other landscape facilities, such as the school gardens, playgrounds, and basketball courts.

2.11 Marble Fairbanks

1 Pre-k and kinder-
  garten
2 Pre-k and k courtyard
3 Administrative offices
4 Health services
5 Discovery center
6 Science lab

7 Library
8 Art room
9 Music room
10 Dining area
11 Gymnasium
12 Interior street
13 Small school 1

14 Small school 2
15 Small school 3
16 Assembly spaces
17 Small school
   courtyards
18 Teacher/parent room

An interior street on the lower level extends the entire
length of the school and connects to ramps leading up
to each of the small schools. Programs that are shared
by each school are on the lower level directly off the
interior street. In addition, the pre-kindergarten and
kindergarten are on this lower level near the main
entrance of the school.

2.12 Winner, South Side

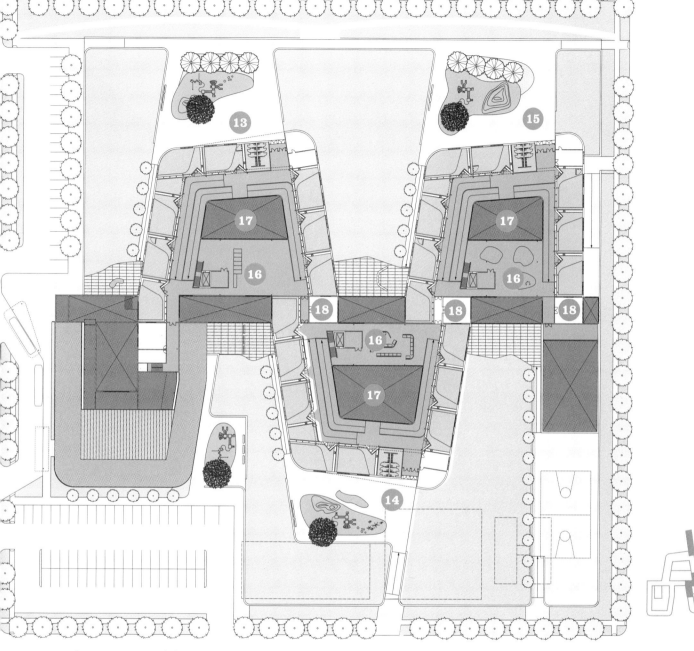

Ramps wrap around the exterior courtyards of each school and connect to the classrooms and assembly spaces. Each school has a secondary entrance that leads to small outdoor playgrounds.

The ability of a building to accommodate change and growth is fundamentally related to its sustainability. This school building has been designed to be able to expand into the site or shift configuration of classes between the small schools. The shaded area of the schematic drawing shows how classrooms can be added to or reassigned for each small school if there is a population change within the overall building.

2.13 Marble Fairbanks

The interior street [1] is the school's major circulation path: it connects the shared program rooms and common spaces — such as the discovery center, library, and dining area — as well as the access ramps leading up to the three small schools.

The upper-level walkway [2] is a shortcut connecting all the small schools. It also bridges the interior street moving from one school's assembly area to another, traveling from the administrative spaces to the gymnasium.

2.14 Winner, South Side

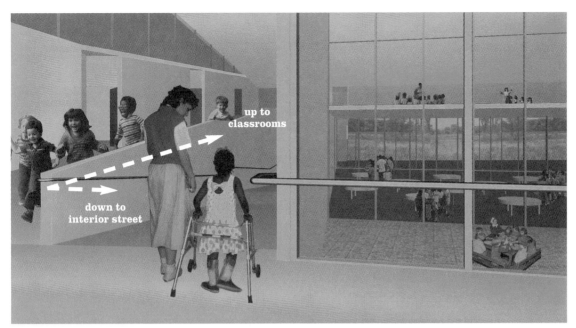

up to classrooms

down to interior street

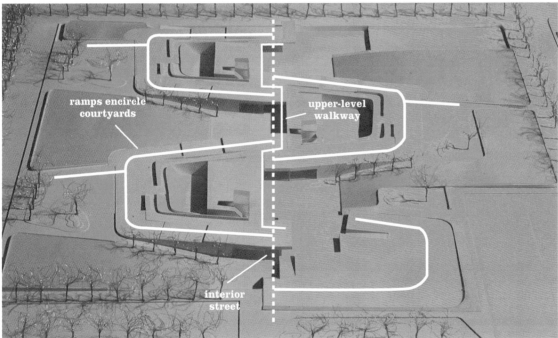

ramps encircle courtyards

upper-level walkway

interior street

The school creates a continuous environment that extends to the edges of the site and engages the neighborhood. The ramps are a continuous thread of movement from sidewalks and play spaces outside to the spiraling circulation around the courtyards.

The schematic drawing shows circulation paths through the school, including the main interior street, from the kindergarten at one end to the gymnasium at the other; the ramps that serve each small school and lead to the upper level; and the upper-level walkway that crosses back and forth over the street, connecting the small schools and assembly areas.

generative spaces

One notable tenet of the small school philosophy is that each school should have its own identity and community with shared goals. To make this possible, the design of this school provides spaces where members of each small school community can gather and interact to generate the vision, spirit, and direction of that school. The architects have provided each small school with one large assembly area or "generative space" on the second floor, overlooking both the interior street and the outdoor courtyards. This assembly area is flexible and allows for each school to define and configure its own needs.

2.16 Winner, South Side

outdoor learning spaces

outdoor courtyards

Outdoor learning spaces are located between each of the small schools on the lower level. Shared programs such as the art room, the science lab, music room, and the discovery center are adjacent to these outdoor spaces.

In addition, a courtyard in the center of each small school brings light to the circulation space and the school's generative space. Each courtyard is landscaped uniquely, providing each school with a different exterior focus.

Jack L. Gordo

Whether students arrive on foot or come by bus or car to the canopy-covered drop-off site, this entrance courtyard is their front door to the school. Jack L. Gordon

Because this area is partly covered and secured by gates, students can spend time here before and after school, during recess in inclement weather, or at other possible times, such as school open-houses, community events, and graduation ceremonies.

In addition to a large open athletic field for soccer and other sports, the school contains two half-courts for basketball and four smaller playgrounds for a variety of activities at all levels, and could include a play wall, a climbing berm, or small-scale features for younger students. A covered playground and a botanical garden provide for additional activities.

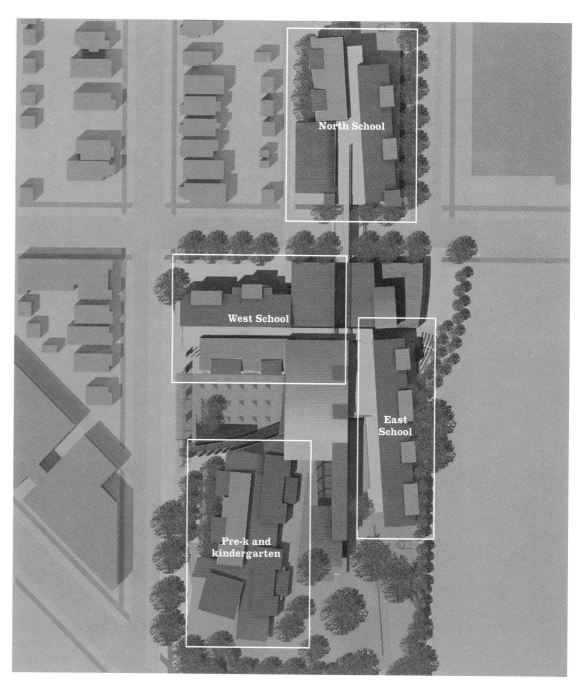

After arriving at the entrance courtyard, pre-kindergartners and kindergartners proceed to a separate but attached one-story building in the southwestern part of the school's site. The entire school complex is built around a primary circulation system that bridges the east-west street bisecting the site and establishes a north-south corridor as the school's primary circulation path, a "main street" anchored by a discovery center at the north end of the school and a library at the south end.

Lower level

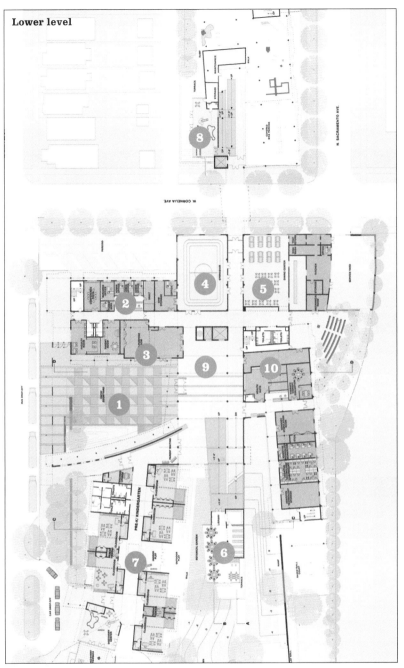

Upper level

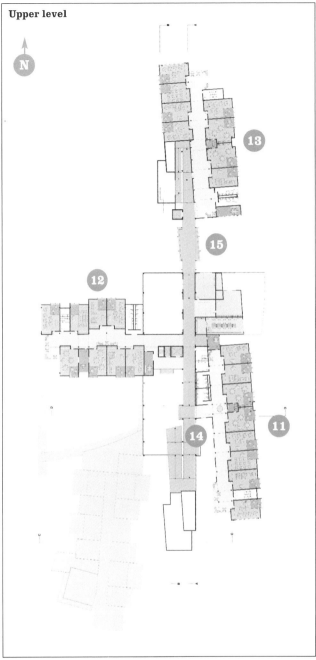

1 Entry courtyard
2 Administration
3 Multipurpose room
4 Gymnasium
5 Dining center
6 Library
7 Pre-k/kindergarten
8 Discovery center
9 Commons/atrium
10 Health and therapy center
11 Small school 1 (grades 1-8)
12 Small school 2
(grades 1-8)
13 Small school 3 (grades 1-8)
14 Ramp/main street
15 Bridge

In addition to the administrative offices and the pre-kindergarten and kindergarten classrooms, other essential components of the school surround the commons area, the geographic heart of the whole facility. The dining center, gymnasium, and multipurpose room may be combined to allow maximum flexibility for school or community functions. The health and therapy center is easily accessible to the entire school community through the commons area.

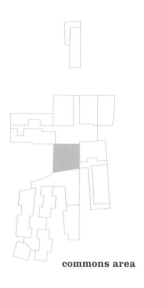

commons area

The central circulation ramp takes students, teachers, and visitors up to three small-school neighborhoods located at different elevations on the second floor. These facilities for grades 1–8 — conceived as the East, West, and North schools — have their own spatial and color-coded identities and their separate entrances along the north-south corridor. All three feature distinctive corridors with unique breakout places, display spaces, and enlarged seating areas with windows at the ends.

The two-story commons area creates a gathering place for the entire school, yet gives students the freedom to navigate its multiple environments, informal nooks, and breakout spaces, as well as more formal assembly places such as the library, dining room, and discovery center. Meanwhile, the school's ramp and "main street" circulation spine are flanked by an open, lattice-like wall that acts as a community billboard.

2.22 Finalists, North Side

The early childhood classrooms support multiple activities with L-shaped floors that teachers can subdivide yet easily supervise. Animated physical play with painting and papier mâché can be conducted around the compact kitchenettes and restrooms, while quieter, more contemplative activity can occur in the nooks at the legs of the L-shaped floors. All classrooms are lighted by windows with direct views, by indirect light from corridor skylights, and by diffused light from clerestories.

2.23 Jack L. Gordon

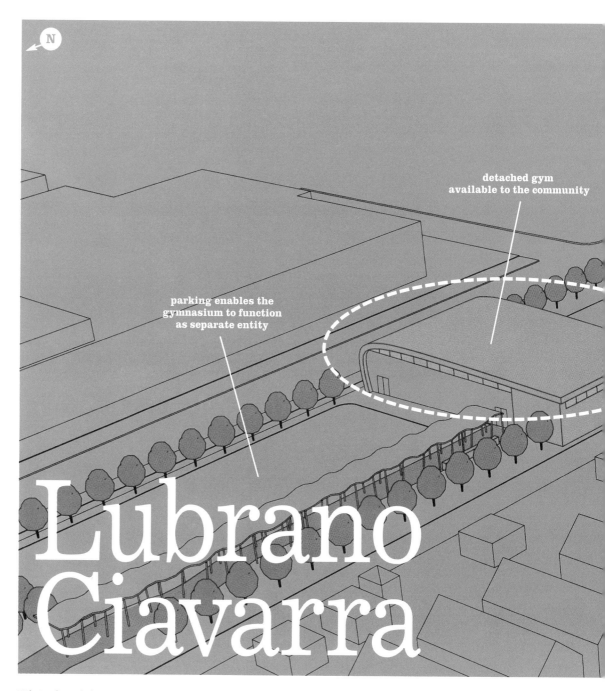

detached gym
available to the community

parking enables the
gymnasium to function
as separate entity

Lubrano Ciavarra

This building was initially imagined as a pair of clasped hands intertwined, "knuckles" exposed. It is composed of four distinct and clearly recognizable parts, which we named "the Umbrella," "the School," "the House," and "the Wall." Lubrano Ciavarra

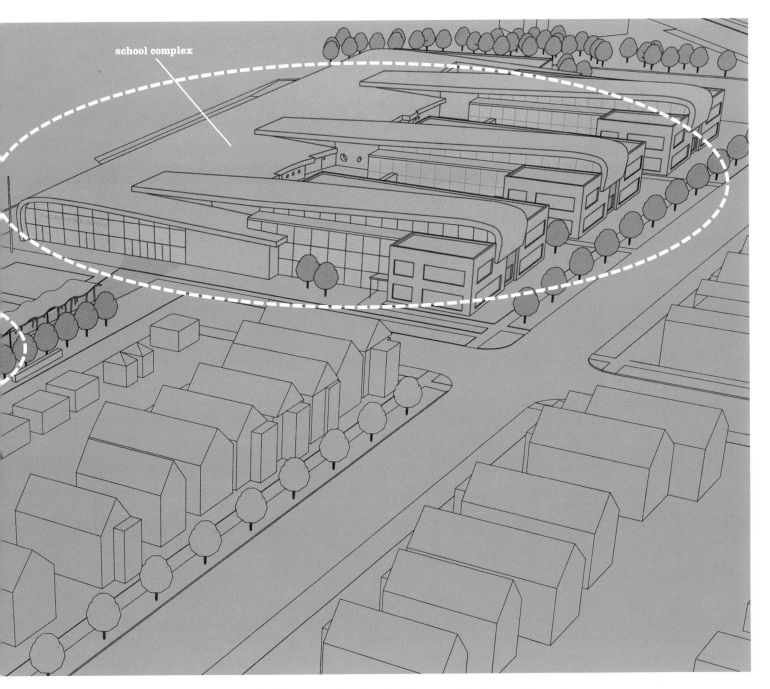

school complex

This aerial view, looking southeast, shows the school complex — containing a preschool and three separate small schools — occupying the southern portion of the site. In the northern part of the site the architects incorporated the existing ball field and playground and added a hard-surface basketball and soccer area, as well as a freestanding gymnasium that could be used separately by the community as a recreational center, a youth center, or a senior center, as needed.

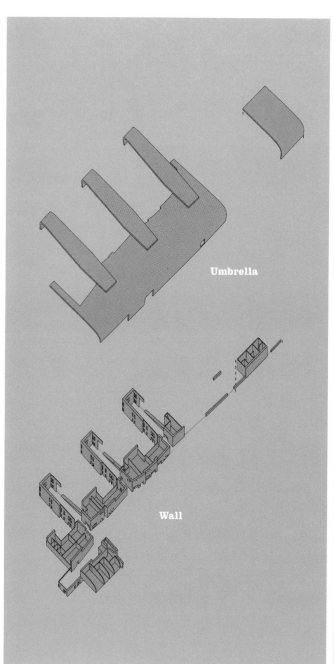

Umbrella

Wall

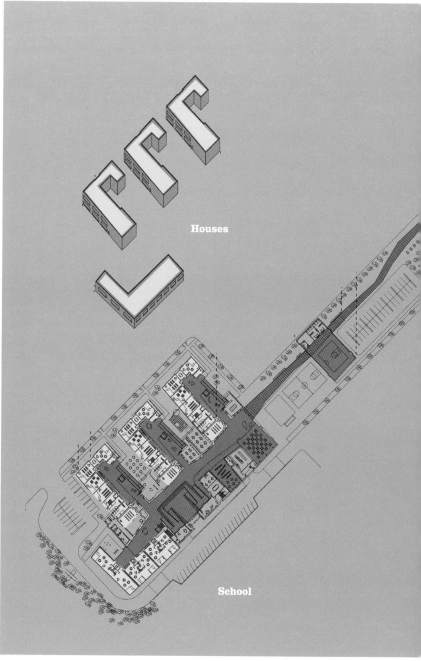

Houses

School

The Umbrella is the building's wrapper or protective shell. Made of corrugated metal panels, the Umbrella unifies the four Houses that together constitute the school complex. The Wall weaves its way through the building, at some points expanding to accommodate special programmed spaces such as the sensory stimulation room, the discovery center, and the art, science, and music rooms. Each of the four Houses constitutes a school-within-the-school.

Finally, the School contains shared common spaces: the main entry and assembly area, the library, the dining center, and the gymnasium. The continuous space of the School fosters shared experiences for students, faculty, and parents during the days, and for other members of the community in the evenings. This multipurpose space also flows into each House, integrating most of the school's activities and all of its common facilities on one level.

2.26 Finalists, North Side

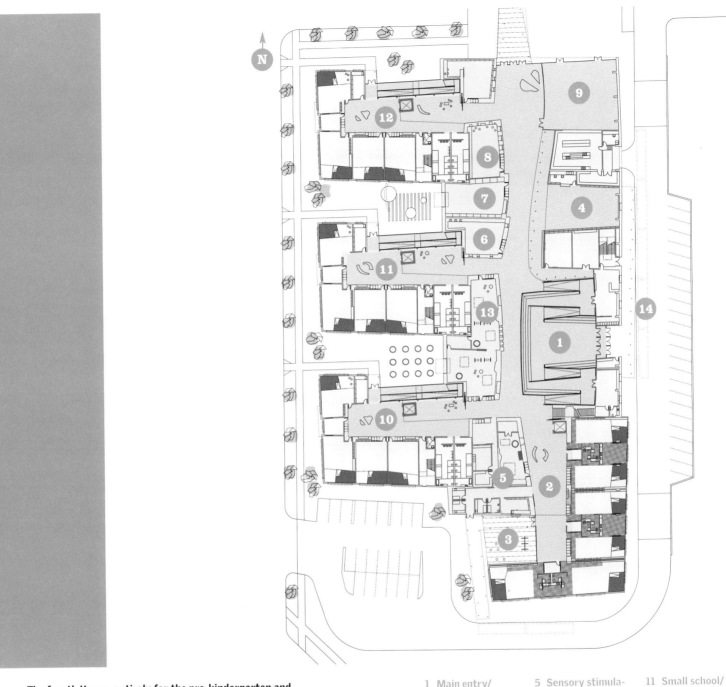

The fourth House, entirely for the pre-kindergarten and kindergarten children, with direct access to the nursing facilities and the sensory stimulation room, is a single-story wing made up of six classrooms. The children in these classes also enjoy a common area as well as direct access to a small, protected, mat-covered playground. Each of the four Houses has its own administrative office that may serve as a visible security post at its exit.

1 Main entry/
assembly area
2 Pre-k/kinder-
garten
3 Pre-k/k play-
ground
4 Library

5 Sensory stimula-
tion room
6 Art room
7 Science lab
8 Music room
9 Dining area
10 Small school/
House 1

11 Small school/
House 2
12 Small school/
House 3
13 Discovery center
14 Bus drop-off

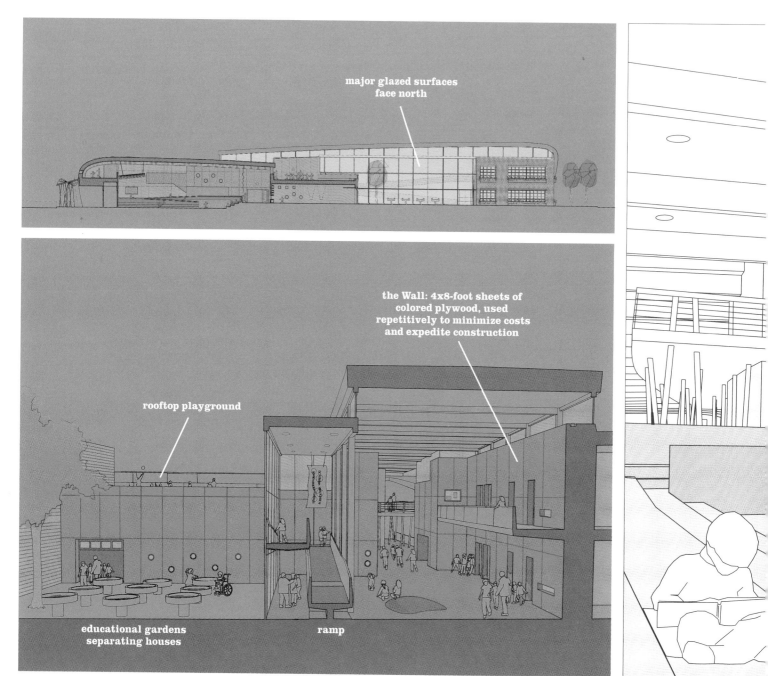

major glazed surfaces face north

the Wall: 4x8-foot sheets of colored plywood, used repetitively to minimize costs and expedite construction

rooftop playground

educational gardens separating houses

ramp

To increase the building's energy efficiency and improve the quality of its environment, all major glazed surfaces, including those of the cafeteria and the ramps in the Houses, face north, to protect against excessive heat gain [top]. Operable windows are also used in all classrooms and administrative spaces to reduce energy loads whenever prevailing winds and moderate temperatures permit.

Each of the three two-story Houses, separated by educational gardens, is unified by an open ramp that links the multipurpose spaces and four classrooms on the main level that serve younger students with the four on the second floor for older students [bottom]. These Houses also have access to a private, rooftop hard-court playground for short, midday recess periods.

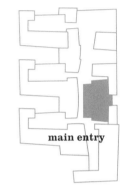

main entry

The main entry and assembly area is one of the most innovative components within the school. By combining ramps with bleacher-type seats, the architects created a "holding area" for children in the morning and afternoon during the drop-off and pick-up periods. Children might do homework here while waiting for a ride or for an after-school activity to commence. At other times of the day this area might contain an entire house of children for an assembly.

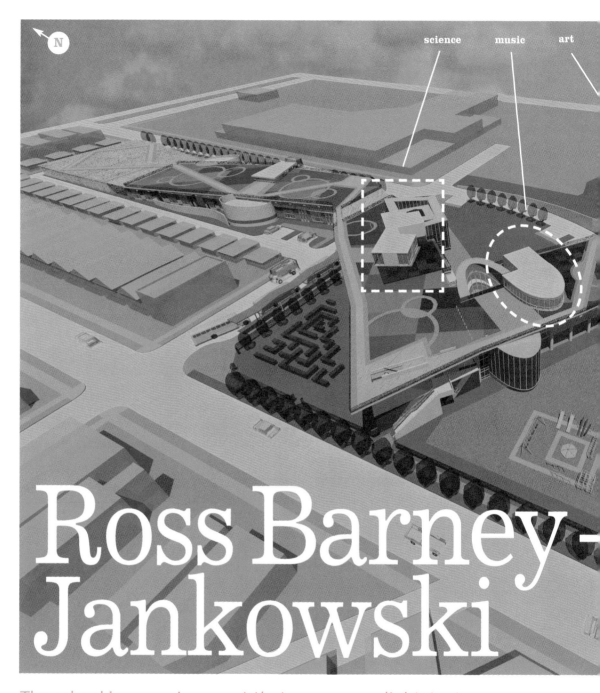

science   music   art

N

Ross Barney Jankowski

The school is an environment that uses space, light, texture, and color to encourage creative and explorative learning. We are trying to design the school that we wanted to attend when we were kids. Ross Barney + Jankowski

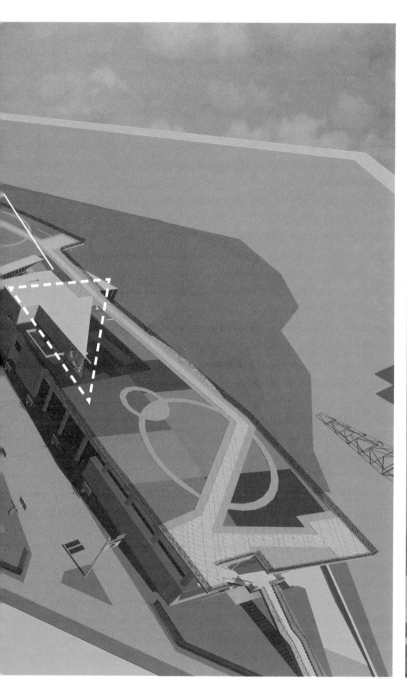

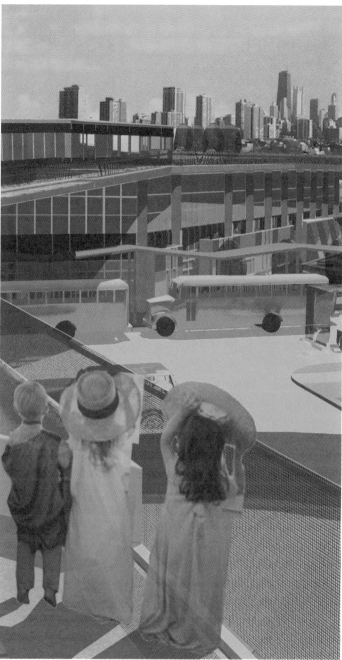

This bird's-eye view, looking north over the entire school complex, shows the garden that has been laid out all along the entire roof of the school, as well as the three special classrooms that sit atop the roof: art (the triangular structure), music (the half-oval room), and science (the rectangular room). Each of the three small schools and the early childhood school has access to this garden level via a ramp, stairway, or elevator.

The rooftop garden level of the school provides an excellent vantage point to look out over the immediate neighborhood and beyond to downtown Chicago in the distance. The garden level is also available for members of the community, who can access it by way of a ramp at the north end of the school property over the trellis-covered parking lot and proceed on the path along its entire length before descending a stairway at the south end of the school.

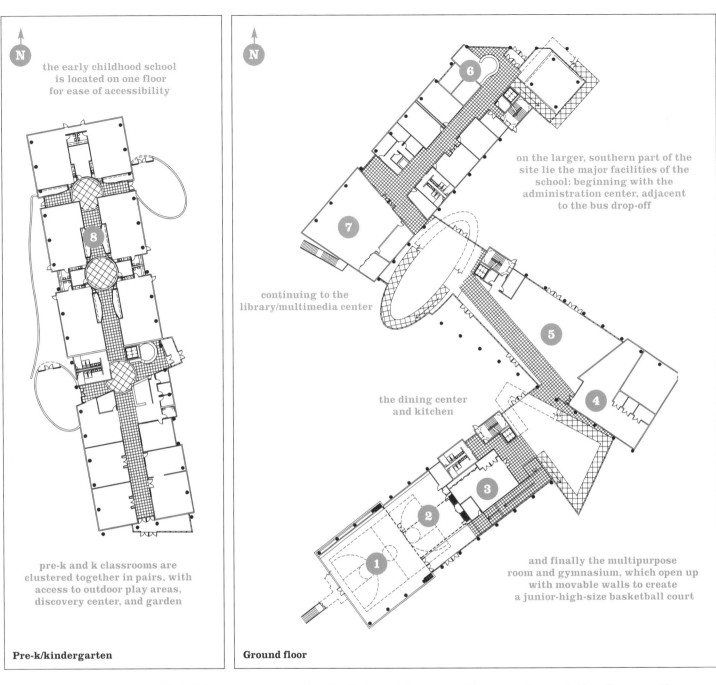

N

the early childhood school is located on one floor for ease of accessibility

N

on the larger, southern part of the site lie the major facilities of the school: beginning with the administration center, adjacent to the bus drop-off

continuing to the library/multimedia center

the dining center and kitchen

pre-k and k classrooms are clustered together in pairs, with access to outdoor play areas, discovery center, and garden

and finally the multipurpose room and gymnasium, which open up with movable walls to create a junior-high-size basketball court

Pre-k/kindergarten

Ground floor

The building wings are arranged on the site to maximize the benefits of solar orientation. East and west elevations are minimal. In addition, the rooftop park, a vegetated roof, will be a legacy for the entire neighborhood and provide many environmental benefits, among them, increased insulation value and energy savings, increased acoustical properties inside the building, protection of the roof membrane for a longer lifespan and lower maintenance costs, and increased aesthetic appeal and property values.

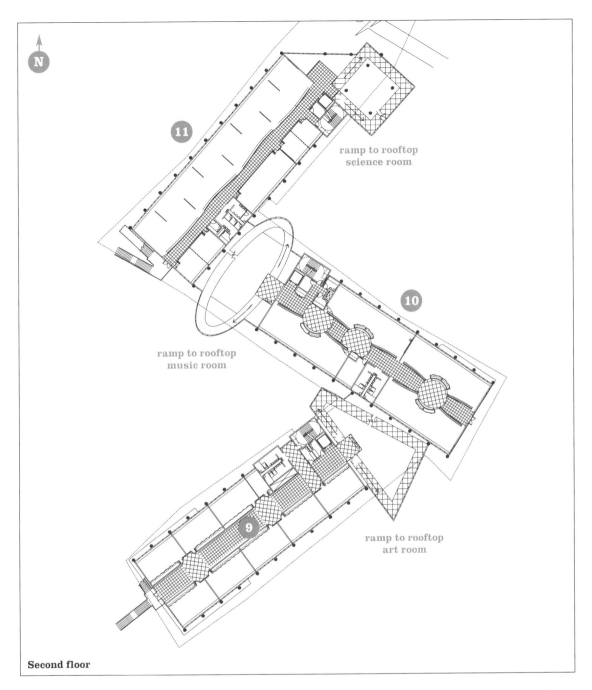

N

11

ramp to rooftop
science room

10

ramp to rooftop
music room

9

ramp to rooftop
art room

Second floor

preschool

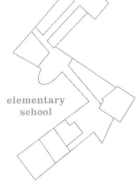

elementary
school

1 Gymnasium
2 Multipurpose room
3 Discovery center
4 Kitchen
5 Dining center
6 Administration
7 Library/multimedia center
8 Pre-k/kindergarten
9 Small school 1
10 Small school 2
11 Small school 3

All three small elementary schools are located on the second floor, recreating what the architects call the intimacy of "living above the store." Each small school has its own wing of the building and its own special entryway and ramp, extending up from the school's main street. The individual small schools are identical in footprint and core requirements, but each of the classrooms can be configured in many different ways, as shown in this plan.

2.33 Ross Barney + Jankowski

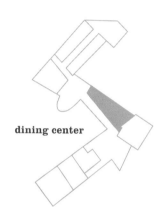

dining center

Finding one's way in this school is easy, as many activities happen on the building's main street, which connects the four separate schools. The cafeteria is a kind of town square, from which the library, the gymnasium, the administrative offices, and the ramps to upper-level schools are all in easy view.

Because each small school has distinct classroom requirements, the individual schools are designed to provide maximum flexibility. The entire space is clear span and has no columns to interfere with classroom layout. A floor-to-ceiling height of eleven feet optimizes natural light in the classrooms. All classrooms have operable windows for natural ventilation and individual control. Almost all classrooms are north-facing, minimizing the need for solar control devices such as shades or blinds.

2.34 Finalists, North Side

structural system allows all
columns to sit outside the school,
keeping the interior space open

The small schools idea is not new, but introducing small schools to dense urban neighborhoods is. Small schools can entail a variety of educational philosophies and curricula. To provide maximum flexibility, the design of this school uses a 68-foot clear span, placing all columns outside the school proper. Marrying innovative programs with new and existing technologies, the architects propose using a cast-in-place post-tensioned concrete structural system commonly used for parking decks.

N

small schools unified under
one shared roof

Borum, Daub
Hyde + Rodd

A school building should balance a dignity of scale on an urban level
with an intimacy of scale on the individual level. Borum, Daubmann, Hyde + Roddier

mann, er

The design strategy for this school derives from the simple diagram of a unifying roof over clusters of smaller buildings. This diagram has remained intact throughout the design process and represents the driving ambition of the proposal: the integration of three small schools into one building, the strength of the whole without a loss of identity of the individual. The scheme is comprised of three types of space: fully internal, semi-internal, and external. This is achieved by the use of a double skin. The outer skin provides weather proofing, security, and a degree of protection from the extremes of temperature that Chicago experiences. The inner skin provides a thermal and acoustical insulation layer to all classrooms and program spaces. Between the two layers is a spatial buffer that is cooled through natural ventilation in the summer and heated passively in the winter.

2.37 Borum, Daubmann, Hyde + Roddier

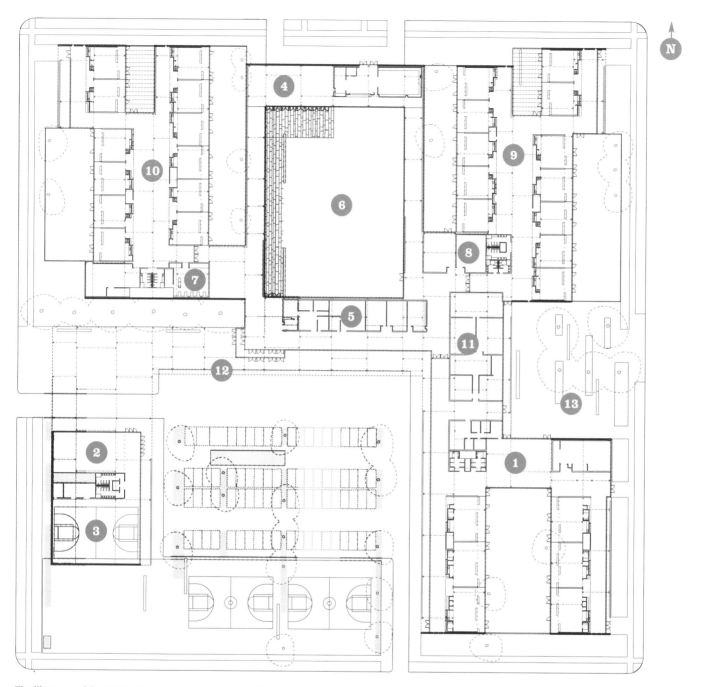

The library, multipurpose room, and gymnasium facilities are located in a semi-autonomous pavilion in the south-west part of the site, allowing easy and secure access to these facilities when the school is closed or public access to them during school hours without disrupting the school's staff and students. Access to these school facilities is covered and on one level.

1 Pre-k/kindergarten
2 Library + multipur-
   pose room
3 Gymnasium
4 Dining area
5 Administration
6 Playground

7 Science room
8 Art room
9 Small school 1
   (grades 1-8)
10 Small school 2
   (grades 1-8)

11 Health center
12 Bus drop-off
13 Community park

2.38 Finalists, South Side

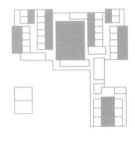

The circulation and assembly spaces for the three schools are between the interior pavilions that house the classrooms and shared facilities. The outer skin thus ensures that all students, teachers, and visitors enjoy free and protected movement from classroom to classroom and school to school. The interior pavilions that contain the classrooms and the various shared facilities such as the art and science rooms maintain a link to the scale of the single-family homes of the surrounding neighborhood. In a similar fashion, the open spaces spread across the school property are seen in relationship to groups of classrooms, just as a house may be seen in relation to its garden. These open spaces create a range of courtyards, gardens, and play areas, large and small. Each classroom is connected to a courtyard, ensuring a means of emergency egress. The dining room overlooks the largest shared play area.

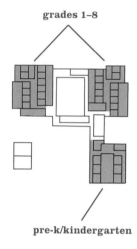

grades 1–8

pre-k/kindergarten

The principal components of the building include prefabricated concrete roof panels on a prefabricated concrete structure, braced with trusses. Exterior enclosure consists of a standard extruded-aluminum storefront system and insulated, precast concrete wall panels. As all weatherproofing is undertaken on the outer roof and walls, the interior pavilions can be composed of simple, insulated, lightweight framing with a plywood and gypsum skin.

Classrooms have been grouped in three clusters: two for grades one through eight, and the third for pre-kindergarten and kindergarten. Each of these clusters includes a shared assembly space for the use of that school. All will enjoy the presence of skylights in the classrooms and common areas.

2.40 Finalists, South Side

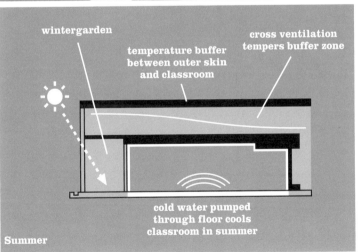

wintergarden

temperature buffer
between outer skin
and classroom

cross ventilation
tempers buffer zone

cold water pumped
through floor cools
classroom in summer

Summer

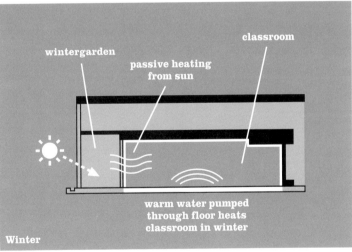

wintergarden

passive heating
from sun

classroom

warm water pumped
through floor heats
classroom in winter

Winter

All classrooms have direct access to an external play area via a glazed wintergarden. These wintergarden zones can be used as breakout spaces for the classrooms, but they also function as a thermal buffer.

This design scheme proposes the use of natural ventilation and passive solar gain, assisted by a radiant slab to achieve comfortable and cost-effective learning environments. Heated water will be pumped through the flooring in the winter and chilled water in the summer.

2.41 Borum, Daubmann, Hyde + Roddier

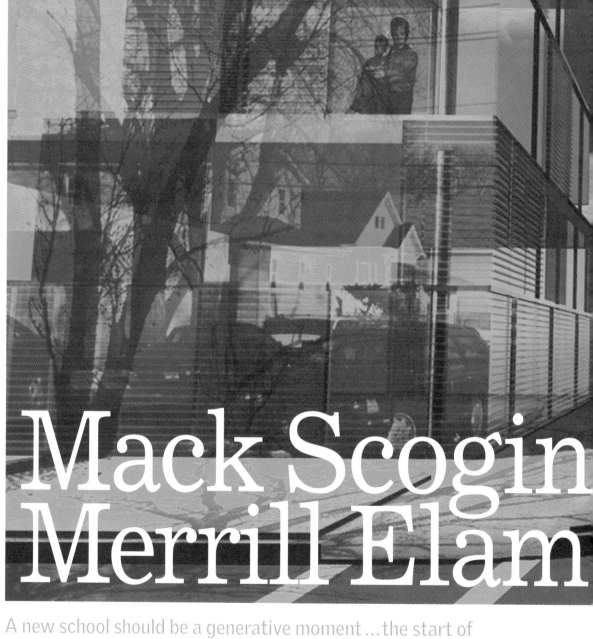

Mack Scogin
Merrill Elam

A new school should be a generative moment…the start of something fresh and invigorating and empowering for the entire community. Mack Scogin Merrill Elam

In a departure from most of the other submissions, the architects of this design propose using only the northern half of the site allotted for the new school, and they recommend preserving and reclaiming for the neighborhood the southern half. Thus, their proposed scheme shows the relocation of homes from the northern half to replace abandoned houses and/or infill empty lots on the southern site and throughout the neighborhood.

While the primary structure is cast-in-place concrete at floors, ramps, bridges, columns, and structural walls, the exterior of the school building combines various types of clear, translucent, and textured glass within an aluminum storefront glazing system. All exterior glass will be insulating glass, tempered as required for safety. Solid wood operable panels will allow for fresh air and cross ventilation in the classrooms, offices, and hallways.

2.43 Mack Scogin Merrill Elam

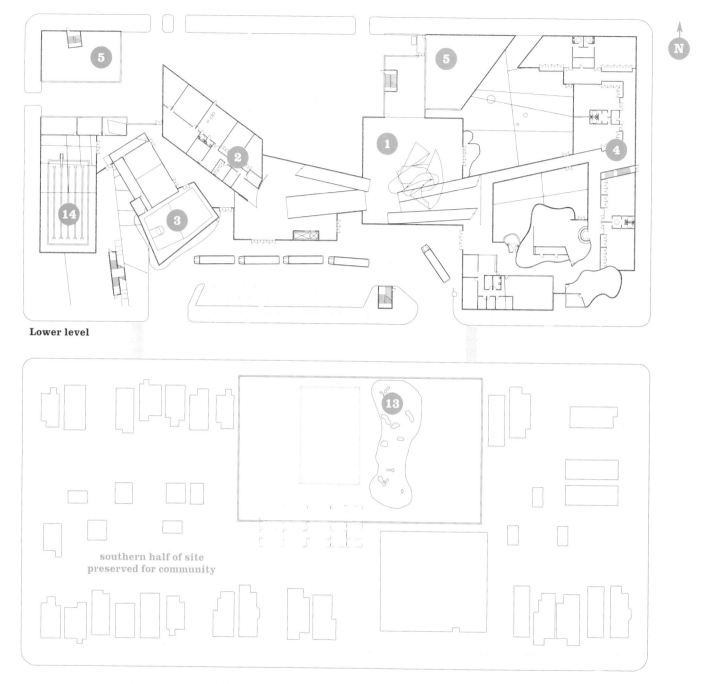

Lower level

southern half of site
preserved for community

The school is distributed on two levels with the three elementary schools for grades one through eight on the upper level, and the commons/cafeteria, the kindergarten and pre-kindergarten, and all other functions on the lower level. In addition, major components of the school have been set around the perimeter of the block, so that the school establishes real contact with the community, perhaps even adding urban spaces for retail to emphasize the school's vital link with the neighborhood.

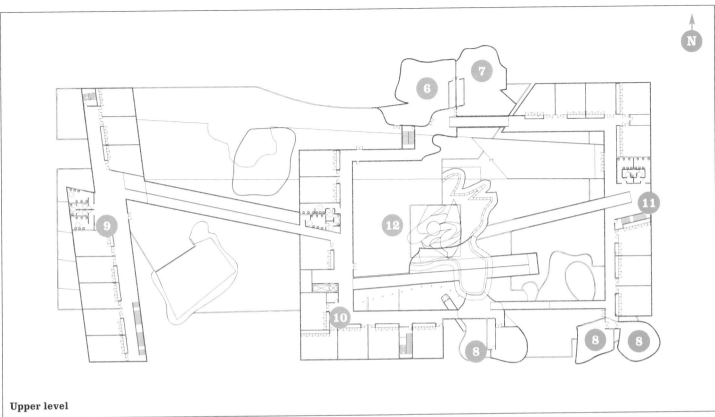

Upper level

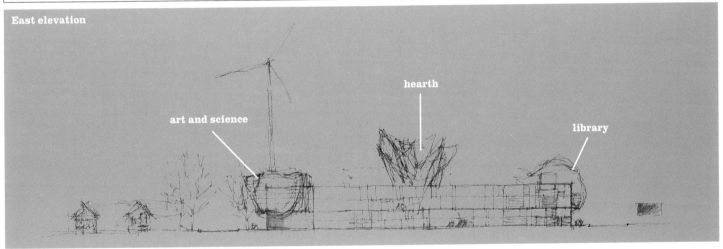

East elevation

art and science

hearth

library

1 Commons +
cafeteria
2 Administration
3 Gym + multipur-
pose room
4 Early childhood
school

5 Retail space
6 Discovery center
7 Library
8 Science, art, +
music rooms
9 Edge School
10 Center School

11 Corner School
12 Hearth
13 Wetland pond
14 Swimming pool
(optional)

Certainly an unusual feature of this school is the presence
of a windmill, for the anticipated use of wind-turbine-
generated power. In addition to this role, the windmill,
along with the wetland pond on the southern half of the
school site, refers back to the historic character of this far
South Side area of Chicago, the home of numerous Dutch
immigrants.

2.45 Mack Scogin Merrill Elam

common area

The three elementary schools on the upper level — identified as the Edge School, the Center School, and the Corner School — are reached by inclined planes that rise very gradually from the central, common area of the school, easily identified by the large, irregularly shaped hearth that forms a defining element of the overall facility.

In sharp contrast to the rectilinear masses of the building, various bulging organic forms define some of the shared spaces in the school, as in the case of the library that extends outward over the sidewalk on the north side of the school, or the art, music, and science rooms on the south side used by the whole student body.

hearth

By pushing important elements to the edge of the site, and making full use of a second level, the architects were able to open up large areas inside the school that serve as play areas or courtyards where students from the separate small schools can interact. In addition to these green spaces, approximately 70% of the roof is either grass play surface over a lightweight soil base or a hardscape play surface of concrete pavers.

2.47 Mack Scogin Merrill Elam

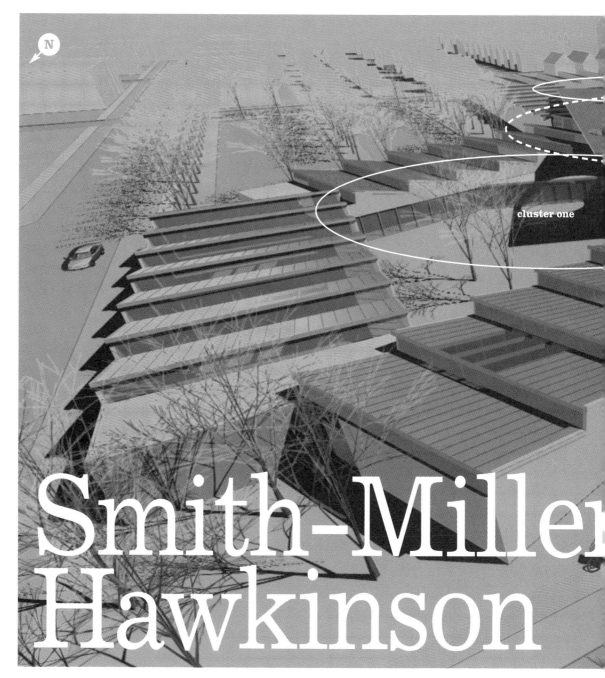

cluster one

Smith-Miller
Hawkinson

Our approach to the design of this school was inspired by the challenge
to create a facility for 800 students that could still provide for smaller
learning environments. The idea of three schools clustered on one site
and on one level became both the formal and philosophical basis for our
design. Smith-Miller + Hawkinson

2.48 Finalists, South Side

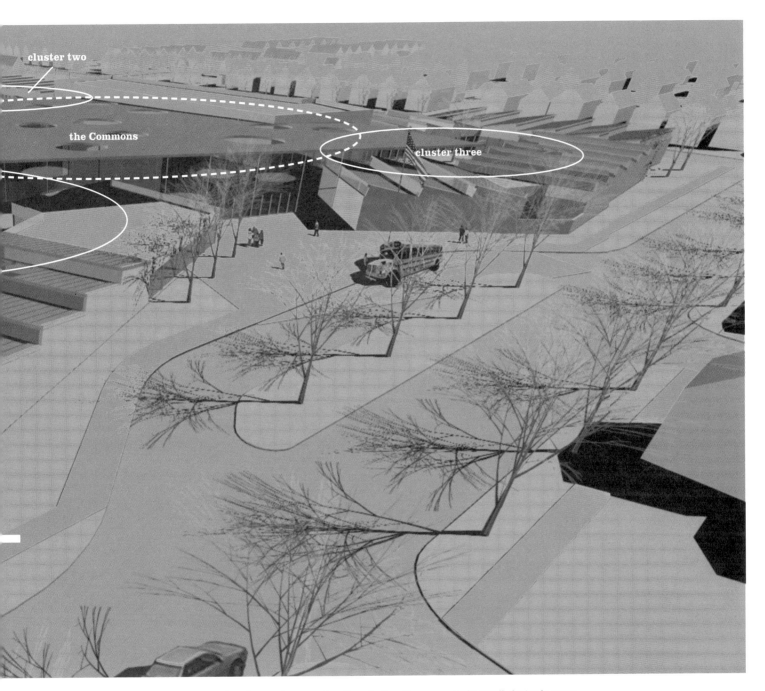

cluster two

the Commons

cluster three

Formally, the concept of a "cluster" operates at a number of levels, from the scale of the individual classrooms to the scale of the overall community. Philosophically, it suggests a way in which something vast can be understood incrementally, similar in many ways to the process of education. Just as the concept of a small cluster became the starting point of the design, so the core of the large cluster – the area called the Commons – became the symbolic center of the entire school. The building block on which the design is based is scaled to correspond to the neighborhood. The roofscape and the long elevations are broken down into smaller pitched-roof components that resonate with the surrounding context.

2.49 Smith-Miller+Hawkinson

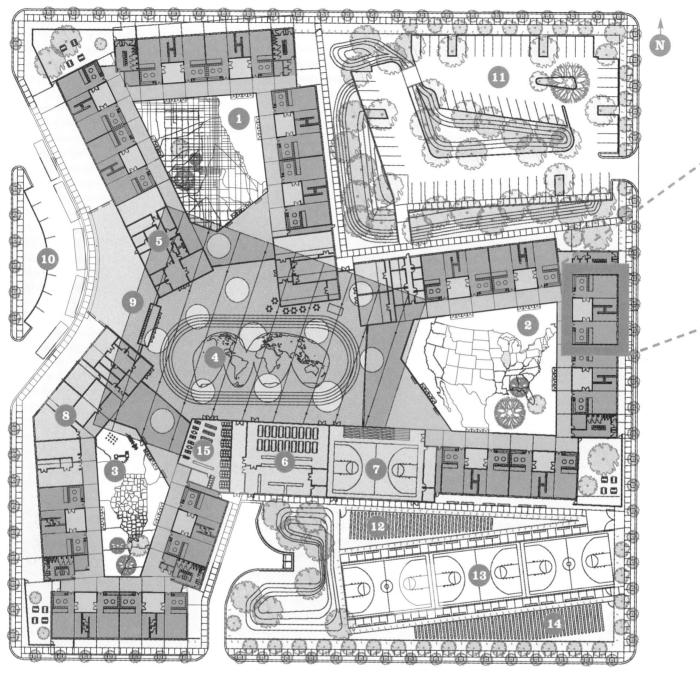

1 Small school 1 courtyard
2 Small school 2 courtyard
3 Small school 3 courtyard
4 Commons
5 Administration
6 Dining
7 Gymnasium
8 Health services
9 Main entry
10 Visitor parking
11 Staff parking
12 School garden
13 Community basketball courts
14 Community garden
15 Library

The building block of each small school is a "classroom cluster": two classrooms grouped around a shared, skylighted greenhouse. Each courtyard has a large-scale map – oriented to true north – integrally embedded in its exterior resilient flooring. Each map is at a different scale and each successively locates the school's site relative to the larger context of the city, state, and country.

N

2.50 Finalists, South Side

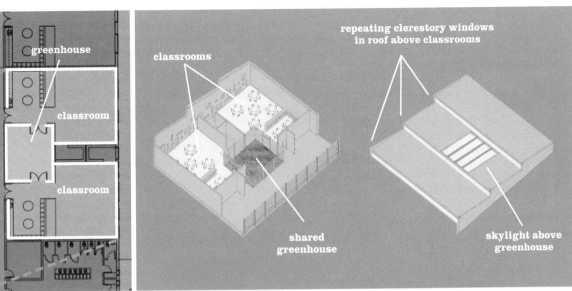

greenhouse

classroom

classroom

classrooms

repeating clerestory windows
in roof above classrooms

shared
greenhouse

skylight above
greenhouse

The greenhouse – visible behind the teacher's desk – can function as an integral part of the school curriculum, a place for class projects in growing and observing, a place to be "outdoors" while still sheltered, a place where two classrooms may share ideas and recreation.

This design, with its repetitive system of north-facing and west-facing clerestory windows, allows for classrooms that are flooded with natural light, have the opportunity for natural ventilation if desired, and possess a strong sense of connection both internally and externally.

2.51 Smith-Miller+Hawkinson

the Commons

The Commons is the heart of the entire school, a place where the three small schools can come together for events such as graduation and a place where the school and the community can interact during school fairs or community forums. The Commons also serves as the entry point for the whole school; from it the glass entry doors to each of the three schools is clearly identifiable. All other shared spaces – administration, music, science, and art rooms, the multipurpose rooms, gymnasium, dining center, library, and health and therapy rooms – are centrally located with entrances directly off the Commons.

courtyards

Each of the three schools has its own central gathering place, an enclosed courtyard, here visible beyond the glass wall of the encircling corridor.

The courtyards can be used for recreation, academic projects, school gatherings, or any spur-of-the-moment-idea a teacher or a class may have. Their principal architectural function is to provide an awareness of orientation, a source of natural light, and a sense of connection.

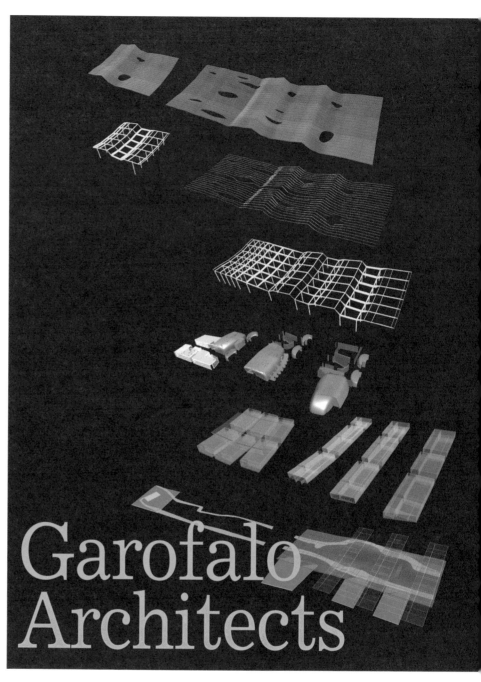

Garofalo Architects

This design attempts to move school design forward through the use of cutting-edge computer technology. Contextuality, for example, is created (using computer graphics) by generating for the roof of the school a reflection of the community's roof-scape. In addition, to participate in the dialogue on universal design, the architects, without resorting to cliches, incorporate differences in spatial character, subtle changes in elevation, and a distinct variety of building forms.

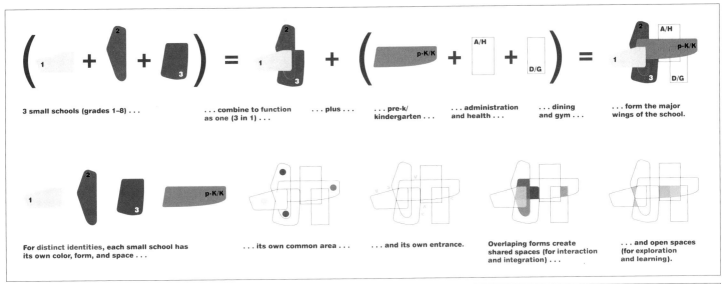

(3 small schools (grades 1–8) . . .) = . . . combine to function as one (3 in 1) . . . . . . plus . . . . . . pre-k/ kindergarten . . . . . . administration and health . . . . . . dining and gym . . . = . . . form the major wings of the school.

For distinct identities, each small school has its own color, form, and space . . .   . . . its own common area . . .   . . . and its own entrance.   Overlapping forms create shared spaces (for interaction and integration) . . .   . . . and open spaces (for exploration and learning).

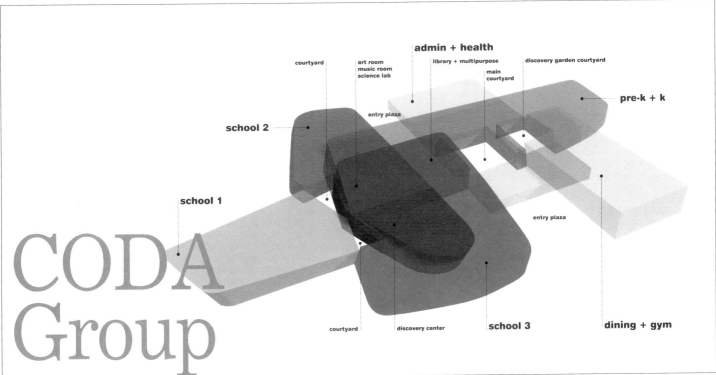

courtyard
art room
music room
science lab
admin + health
library + multipurpose
main courtyard
discovery garden courtyard
entry plaza
pre-k + k
school 2
school 1
entry plaza
CODA Group
courtyard
discovery center
school 3
dining + gym

The architect's diagrams are extremely effective teaching tools and visual depictions of the logic behind the school's organization. The diagrams display a clarity of volumetric expression and each distinctive shape symbolizes the identity of one of the small schools within the larger complex. The overall concept successfully incorporates sophisticated graphic design in order to assist with navigation through the school.

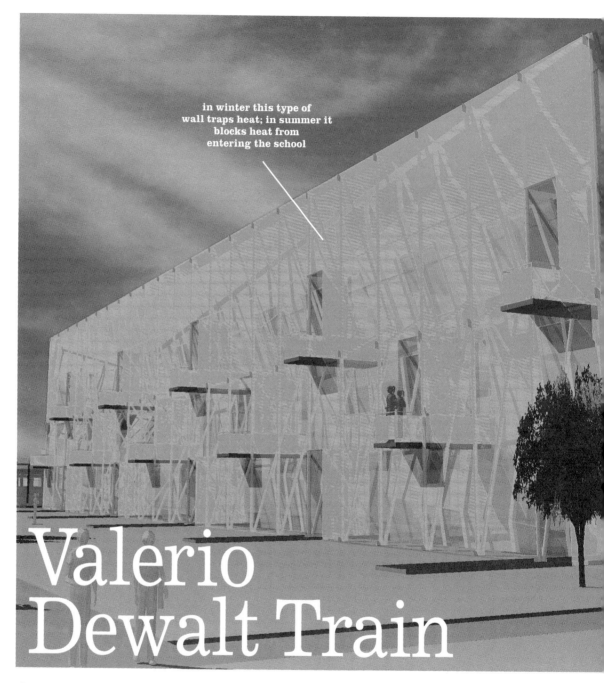

in winter this type of
wall traps heat; in summer it
blocks heat from
entering the school

Valerio Dewalt Train

This design exhibits an elegant architecture that commu-
nicates the futurism of the twenty-first century. Its
energy conservation plan is especially notable, not least
for its inclusion of a solar wall. The glass-faced Trombe
wall along the entire southern exterior is part of an effort
to use passive solar features to reduce the building's
overall energy use. Thus, this architecture exhibits an
innovative use of green design techniques.

two circular discovery centers at diagonally opposite corners uniquely characterize the school

a secured, definable perimeter is established around the building

Jeffrey Funke

This design exhibits a good sense of spatial hierarchy and an effective use of the site. The design suggests the possibilities of integrating indoor and outdoor space. It incorporates specific, desirable features, such as several protected interior playgrounds, while allowing for generous ball fields and other playing areas.

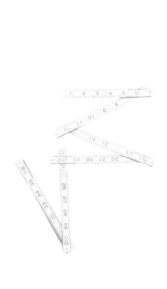

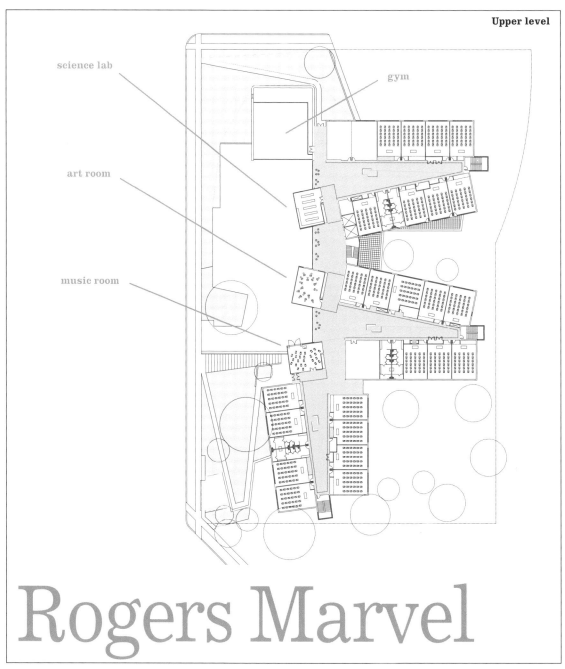

science lab

gym

art room

music room

Rogers Marvel

This compact solution offers a variation on the finger theme with a clustering of community spaces, such as the gym and library, and an elegant treatment of the entrance side of the school. A specialty room at the entrance to each hallway marks the individual small schools in this design. Images of art, science, or music could be viewed along each hallway, and students could appreciate each other's artwork and projects. From the street, these classrooms would become display cases of student work for the community to observe.

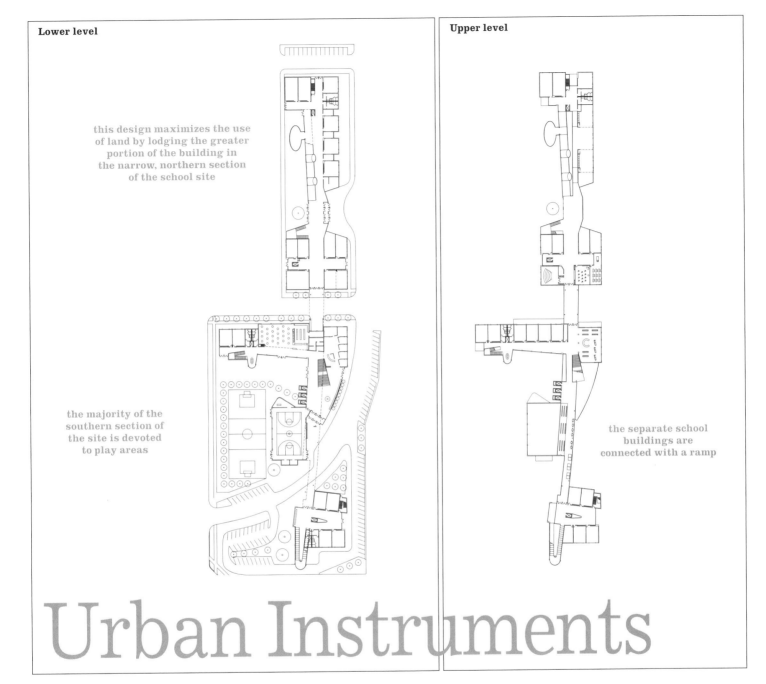

this design maximizes the use of land by lodging the greater portion of the building in the narrow, northern section of the school site

the majority of the southern section of the site is devoted to play areas

the separate school buildings are connected with a ramp

Urban Instruments

This design is full of life and acknowledges that children need to play and have fun. The presentation is playful and inviting and expresses the natural energy of children and the possibilities for liveliness within the design of the school itself. The design also uses unique ideas such as conical story-telling rooms accessible by ramp and ramp lookout plazas topped by charming funnel-shaped structures.

2.59

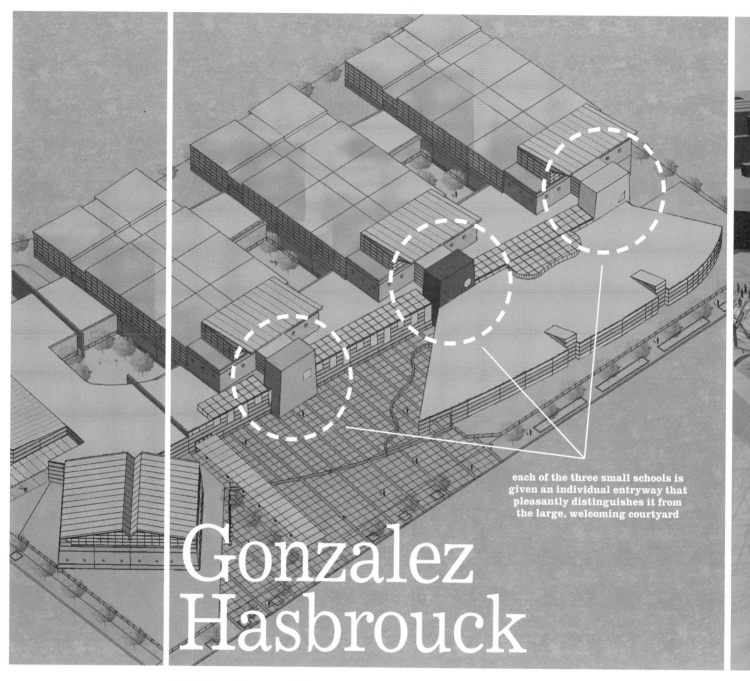

each of the three small schools is given an individual entryway that pleasantly distinguishes it from the large, welcoming courtyard

Gonzalez Hasbrouck

This design achieves a good balance between creating discrete small-school communities and providing accessible areas such as the gymnasium, dining room, and commons for functions that serve the larger community. The outdoor student commons and play area and the indoor foyer areas create a deliberate space of arrival at each small school. The proposed amphitheater on the northern portion of the site by the parking lot offers another interesting possibility for outdoor community use.

clerestory windows run
the length of the school

Griffin Enright

Given the context of the school's immediate neighborhood, the architects of this proposal displayed a bold approach to school design, using transparency to create a sense of approachability and availability of the school. The design emphasizes glass and light, employing skylights and clerestory windows, as well as areas of glass along the playground, and at the individual school entryways.

while traditional classrooms are enclosed
and isolated from other students and
from the outside, this classroom design tried
to break through such stereotypes by
opening the classroom to the outside world
through access to a small alcove

STL Architects

The architects of this design focused on the individual
classroom unit, and grouped them in pairs so that they
could share elements such as lockers, office/conference
rooms, and common areas. They also varied the design
and position of windows to acknowledge the different
heights of the students.

design exhibits an intense integration of
the landscape with the built structure

Frederic Schwartz

The thoroughly landscaped roof of this design acts as a
gathering place for the school and the community and
could feature gardens or other related projects benefiting the school's curriculum.

window boxes

von Weise Associates

A grand ramp is the power that fuels this simple design. The design presupposes that everyone will utilize the ramp to access the entrances to the three individual small schools. No ramp is necessary to enter the first-floor pre-kindergarten and common areas such as the gymnasium and dining room. The building's exterior treatment includes window boxes on the first- and second-floor levels, as well as a playful, textured surface on the kindergarten entrance, all of which adds a special identity to each school while bringing the school closer to the outside community.

Policies and Principles

The Promise and Politics of Small Schools

Susan Klonsky, Director of Development
Small Schools Workshop, University of Illinois at Chicago

A recent large-scale study showed that small schools – of about 350 students at the elementary level or a maximum of 600 at the secondary level – could largely counteract the negative effects of poverty on student achievement, specifically for low-income children and students of color.[1] This data shows exactly why small school size is not merely an architectural issue but also a social justice issue. Today, throughout the United States, there are hundreds of new public schools that are small on purpose: not small because of high dropout rates, but small by design. The movement toward small public schools has been driven by concerns about safety and student achievement, and by a growing recognition – now confirmed by research – that huge, impersonal institutions are the worst possible places in which to educate our young. The big, factory-style schools of the last century are antithetical to strong community and individual identity. The typical large high school, ranging from 1,300 to 3,000 students, may require a faculty of between 120 and 200 adults, and, ironically, in such large staffs, teachers rarely have the opportunity to collaborate meaningfully with each other, let alone to get to know their students well. For years the small schools movement has had to make do with existing buildings that are renovated or retrofitted to meet the needs of small school programs. Only rarely since the rise of this new trend in public education has a new public school been designed specifically to accommodate one or more small schools within its walls.

It should come as no surprise that the value of small schools is something the wealthy have always known. Naturally, private prep schools are small by virtue of their desire for exclusivity, but they are also kept small because such a size enables students and a specific culture of learning to flourish. Likewise, residents of affluent suburbs insist on small class sizes for their children, no matter what the cost. Indeed, small class size has long been recognized as a hallmark of good schools. But new research has proven in unambiguous fashion that the sheer institutional size of large schools weighs against student achievement. In fact, school size is one of the most important factors determining the rate of achievement by school.

In the coming decade we will spend over $500 billion dollars on new school construction in this country. Yet, despite all the evidence in favor of small schools, nearly all of this money will go to the building of mega-schools, bigger than the ones they replace. Despite a spate of architectural competitions across the country, many of the best designs for schools will never be built. Aesthetics is not what drives decision-making, nor is educational research nor social justice for communities where modern public schools are urgently needed. Instead, what drives large-scale building is, all too often, political consideration, patronage, and money. The enduring myth of economies of scale persists in persuading policy-makers that they cannot afford to build smaller, when, in fact, they can ill afford to build big. A large physical plant requires a multimillion dollar investment in security devices, traffic management, and personnel to guard its multiple entry doors, all of which can lead to a highly militarized environment with a pervasive police presence, metal detectors, and video surveillance. Hardly the feeling of a homey, stimulating, and welcoming learning environment.

The effort to create smaller and more personalized public schools is a design problem now being taken up not only by educators but by architects and planners. They have come face-to-face with the question: Can a school be at once large enough to offer adequate resources to all students, and small enough to provide them a safe, nurturing, and comfortable environment? Can a school that is small by design accommodate the breadth of experiences and encounters we want our students to share? This is the tension we face as we redesign and rebuild public schools for a new generation of children. Identifying a balance and a social approach to the physical size of schools can allow us to imagine schools in a new way. But a top-down design process that omits the active participation of parents, students, community members, and teachers will merely perpetuate the building of impersonal schools that characterize a bygone era.

One exciting exception to conventional practice is the Little Village High School, located in Chicago's Mexican immigrant community. This densely populated, underserved community has no public high school of its own. Students here drop out of Chicago high schools at a rate of about 66 percent. In 2001, parents and community activists conducted a lengthy sit-in and hunger strike on an empty lot to call public attention to the desperate need for a high-quality local high school. Ultimately their efforts triumphed; the parents and organizers succeeded in winning a commitment from the Chicago Public Schools to build not only a new high school for this port-of-entry area, but a future-minded "multiplex" of four individual small high schools that will share one brand-new facility. Each floor of the building will house a unique school. Each small high school will have its own curricular theme or focus (such as the fine and performing arts, the health sciences, international languages, and so on). All four schools will share certain common facilities, such as the gymnasium, swimming pool, and cafeteria. When this school finally opens its doors in 2005, it will be the product of a highly participatory four-year design process, in which the architects have worked closely with community leaders and educators to ensure that the physical design matches as closely as possible the ideals of the planners, and that the educators and parents are well aware of all the design options and possibilities. The school will embody traditional, clearly identifiable Mexican design elements, as well as state-of-the-art technology and safety features. Finally, say community organizers, this neighborhood is getting the school it needs and deserves.

A Matter of Justice

The contemporary movement for small public schools is rooted in the civil rights movement in the South during the 1960s. The "freedom schools" and "citizenship schools" in Mississippi and Alabama were established by civil rights workers to educate children who had been forced out of the segregated public schools. Black sharecroppers were dismissed from their jobs and kicked off their farms for attempting to register to vote. As part of a pattern of collective punishment, their children were suspended from the very schools that the descendants of slaves had attended since Reconstruction. Civil rights organizers put the freedom schools to work – keeping the young people occupied, preparing them to be activists in the movement, and providing lessons in literacy, politics, and culture when their public schools were shuttered. At the height of the civil rights movement in 1964, there were over 80 such freedom schools throughout the Deep South.[2] These schools had no buildings of their own: they convened in public parks, farmyards, and churches, but their makeshift physical circumstances were offset by the powerful sense of community and shared purpose that brought them into being.

In designing schools today, the conditions and criteria are different. We are not producing students destined for the assembly line. Instead, we seek two basic relationships that change the defining dynamics of schools: first, effective schools find ways *to make each child visible* and well-known to the adults who will teach her; second, effective schools offer each teacher a place in *a strong professional community of educators*. Neither of these two big relationships can be attained in large, impersonal institutions, where anonymity is the order of the day. Individualized instruction and the ability to work in small groups as part of a team are hallmarks of small-schools education. Spaces that afford both individual and small-group work are key elements in planning such schools.

What can be done to make the policy shift necessary to invest in such designs? First, communities must know the value of small schools. The Little Village parents experienced these values firsthand as their children attended a new, small, innovative public elementary school in their neighborhood. They sought to continue that intimate, purposeful learning environment for their children *on into high school*, but they found no such high school existed. Second, when new school bonds are floated and new public investments are planned, communities must mobilize to demand human-scale schooling. To avoid building new schools that repeat the errors of the past, people need to look at successful design efforts like those in North Port, Florida, and Mansfield, Ohio, where new high schools have been planned as complexes of small and specialized small schools in shared facilities. Unfortunately, most communities rely on professional school designers to create the plan, with perhaps a smattering of input from the teachers. In Cicero, Illinois, Unity Junior High, which opened in 2002, was built for 4,000 students in grades 6–8 simply because a state construction grant was available and the district opted for the maximum amount of funds. An open, public exploration of the options and possibilities might have averted this mistake. But without an informed public, such monstrosities are erected unchallenged, despite massive evidence that warehousing adolescents in giant schools is a recipe for increased rates of violence and academic failure.

An Open Process

Clearly, a good building is not enough to make a good school, and a wonderful building with all the bells and whistles cannot guarantee a good education. Whether a school is physically pretty or ugly, luxurious or spartan, will in the final analysis have little to do with how it makes people feel about education. Instead, it has to do with whether those most affected by the school are at the table, and it has to do with the design's ability to provide a number of components that are visible in the designs featured in this book: a strong community gathering place, be it a hearth or an all-purpose room; personal learning spaces within the whole, manifesting respect for privacy and for the individual; navigability and simplicity for the comfort, order, and safety they supply; room and respect for the services and programs that support family involvement, health, and community ties; outreach and openness to the community, to ensure an amicable and permeable relationship between the school and its surroundings; and a floor plan, grid, or other mechanism that lends itself intentionally and easily to division into small learning communities within the whole.

A good design is a just design, and a just design addresses the specific needs of the community the school will serve. An open process that engages the best thinking and ideals of many people – not just the architects, but the teachers, the parents, and the students as well – is the most important safeguard of a good design: coming together around a common vision with a clear-cut set of desires and principles. An open process can go far to ensure that the rights of the neediest communities are addressed; that big obsolete schools go the way of the dinosaurs; and, finally, that the new small spaces we create offer big opportunities for learning that go far beyond the classroom walls.

1 Craig Howley, Marty Strange, and Robert Bickel, *Research about School Size and School Performance in Impoverished Communities* (Charleston, West Virginia: ERIC Clearinghouse on Rural Education and Small Schools, 2000).

2 Len Holt, *The Summer That Didn't End* (New York: DaCapo Press, 1992).

Small Schools, Now

Alexander Polikoff, Senior Staff Counsel
Business and Professional People for the Public Interest

Paul Grogan, formerly of Harvard and now head of The Boston Foundation, is a world-class optimist about American cities. Of Grogan's recent book, *Comeback Cities*, Tom Brokaw says, "Read this and re-gain your hope."

Yet even the optimist Grogan acknowledges that there is an "albatross" in the picture – the exodus of the working and middle classes to the suburbs. In central cities, Grogan says, where markets and incomes are improving, the residents who are moving back are the childless and, occasionally, families with higher incomes who can afford private schooling for their children: "There is no evidence of a significant move by working and middle-class families with children who have choices to stay in cities." Grogan continues:

> The leadership in nearly every older city and neighborhood will tell you, first off, that the principal barrier they face in keeping current residents in inner-city neighborhoods and recruiting new ones is the schools ... Those who have any economic choice have stopped tolerating [the public school].[1]

Of the five Chicago Public Schools Design Competition criteria, only one implicates an approach to education reform. Why, among the myriad of proffered reforms of recent decades, is the personalized learning environment of small schools accorded this preeminent place? A little history will explain.

The 1983 report of the National Commission on Excellence in Education, *A Nation at Risk,* said that the quality of American education was so poor that had it been imposed by a foreign nation it would have been deemed an act of war.[2] Many states responded with serious efforts to improve public schools, such as stricter graduation requirements, higher teacher salaries, and minimum competency tests for teachers. By the end of the decade, however, these "first-wave" reforms had produced little improvement in students' learning.

A second wave called "restructuring" followed, based upon two themes: first, centralized bureaucratic systems were not achieving results; and, second, every school was unique – a combination of personalities, relationships, and physical circumstances that needed continual fine-tuning and therefore a large measure of local, "on-site" control. School-based management (SBM), the most widely practiced of restructuring techniques, involved devolution to the school level of some authority previously tightly held by the central office regarding instruction, budget, personnel, and school organization.

When SBM failed to achieve hoped-for results, a modified second-wave strategy began to gain prominence. While adhering to devolution, the modified strategy focused on implementation: what should be done with the devolved authority? Yet the answer that emerged – to create "personalized learning environments" – flew directly in the face of a half century of American educational thinking during which widespread school consolidation had taken place. By the end of the twentieth century, the number of school districts and schools had declined 87 percent and 69 percent, respectively, while the average number of students per district and per school skyrocketed.

Unfortunately, the consolidation movement took us in precisely the wrong direction. An impressive body of research has now made it clear that small schools, not big ones, provide the kind of environment within which learning can best take place. With drumbeat consistency, this research sounds the small schools refrain. A review of more than 100 studies conducted over the past dozen years describes as "remarkably unequivocal" the conclusion that students do better in smaller schools. Another review of the evidence concludes that the superiority of small schools has been established "with a clarity and level of confidence rare in the annals of education research." Indeed, so strong has the accumulating evidence become that one researcher says, "There is enough evidence now [of the benefits of small schools] – and of the devastating effects of large size on substantial numbers of youngsters – that it seems morally questionable not to act on it."[3]

The details are as impressive as the conclusions. Study after study shows that the benefits of small schools suffuse the entire schooling enterprise, including the "payoff" criterion of higher graduation rates. One study concludes that while the best predictor of pupil achievement is what most observers would expect, that is, socio-economic status, the next best predictor is school size.[4] Continuing down the list of performance measures, the now-demonstrated benefits of small schools include lower rates of disciplinary problems, truancy, and dropouts, higher levels of parent and community involvement, higher levels of teacher satisfaction, and even lower costs per student graduated. Small schools have also been shown to be particularly effective with lower-income and minority students. These are the harvests we reap when we turn away from oversized schools where, as Chicago Public Schools CEO Arne Duncan says, "students feel anonymous and [believe] that no one cares about them."

Theodore Sizer is considered by many to be America's most famous education reformer, his Coalition of Essential Schools (CES) among the most effective of broad school reform efforts. CES, founded in 1984, has been built around nine essential principles, and schools wishing to join it must subscribe to each of them. Yet after a decade of work, a tenth, "corollary" principle emerged. In the words of researcher Kathleen Cushman, it is that "the other [nine] principles are nearly impossible to achieve in big schools."[5] Philanthropy evidently agrees. The Bill and Melinda Gates Foundation has invested more than a quarter of a billion dollars in small schools, and other foundations following suit include Carnegie, Ford, and Kellogg. In addition, during 2001 and 2002 Congress set aside over $250 million for school districts wanting to create smaller schools. At the level of research and analysis, therefore, it may be said that small schools are now widely embraced as the long-sought counterattack against the figurative act of war to which *A Nation at Risk* had pointed.

Yet, "doing" small schools is not easy. "Small schools" means more than small size. It means also a cohesive, self-selected faculty supported by like-minded parents, a coherent curricular or pedagogical focus that provides a continuous educational experience across a range of grades, an inclusive admissions policy that gives weight to student and parent commitments to the school mission, and substantial autonomy as to curriculum, budget, organization, personnel, and other matters. Fashioning an institution that possesses these characteristics is a daunting task. Small schools are not a panacea. Like big schools, they can be bad schools. The claim for small schools is that they provide an environment within which the daunting task is more likely to be performed.

"Substantial autonomy" may be the biggest challenge of all facing small schools. Power-sharing does not come naturally to most persons and institutions. Witness the resistance to charter schools, most of which are small. The bureaucratic midsections of central systems often strongly resist change even when word from the top supports it. Small schools, supposedly granted "autonomy," frequently find themselves expected to comply with rules – designed for the convenience of the central system or embedded in union contracts – that are incompatible with small schools operational arrangements.

Enter the Chicago Public Schools Design Competition with its requirement that entries be "sensitive to small school design." Separate space appears to be essential to achieving real autonomy. It is not the only requisite, but it is a necessary one. It is difficult to imagine teachers and parents working together to make a small school "theirs," if their school is but a department of a larger institution that does not exercise fundamental control over its own physical space. The integrity of separate space is a threshold need.

This is why one of the five Chicago Design Competition criteria focuses on space – buildings designed (at feasible cost) to accommodate the structure and educational philosophy of small schools. Buildings, as the competition criterion states, "should be organized in a way that allows the same group of teachers to work with the same small group of students over their entire educational experience, from first to eighth grade." Thus, the sponsors of the competition believed, design could best make its contribution to education by fostering the personalized learning environment that is our most hopeful avenue for education reform.

Nudged perhaps by this competition, we are beginning to move in that direction. In June 2002 the Chicago Board of Education announced a capital program that included the construction of two new high schools. A *Chicago Sun-Times* article, headlined "New High Schools Will Accent Thinking Small," reported, "For the first time, the schools will be designed for the express purpose of being subdivided into four small schools, each with its own curriculum."[6]

Sizer says schools that go down to a human scale see the results. Schools are more likely to go down to a human scale when they are given a physical space that is designed for the human scale. Among its most valuable outcomes, the Chicago Public Schools Design Competition shows both the educational and architectural establishments that it is feasible to go down to the human scale and create the personalized learning environments that at long last will enable public education to thrive.

1 See Paul S. Grogan and Tony Proscio, *Comeback Cities: A Blueprint for Urban Neighborhood Revival* (Boulder, Colorado: Westview Press, 2000).

2 The report is available on the World Wide Web at http://www.ed.gov/pubs/NatAtRisk/.

3 Mary Anne Raywid, "Examining the Case for Small Schools," unpublished paper, 1997.

4 See Kathleen Cotton, "School Size, School Climate, and Student Performance," Northwest Regional Educational Laboratory, 1996.

5 Kathleen Cushman, "Why Small Schools Are Essential," *Horace* 13:3 (January 1997), pp. 1–7.

6 Fran Spielman, "New High Schools Will Accent Thinking Small," *Chicago Sun-Times*, June 26, 2002.

Universal Design: Small Schools That Fit the Whole Community

David K. Hanson, Commissioner
Mayor's Office for People with Disabilities

Denise R. Arnold, AIA, Program Director, Architectural Services Unit
Mayor's Office for People with Disabilities

John H. Catlin, AIA
Partner, LCM Architects, LLC

Shelley A. Sandow, M.A.
ADA Compliance Consultant

Have you ever felt that the built environment or some personal product was particularly difficult to manage or required an excessive amount of effort to use? After a softball or soccer game that left you stiff, for instance, have you been stymied in trying to rise from a chair that lacks arms to push against? Have you ever been shown to a booth at a coffee shop and taken your seat at a table about level with your collarbone? Or perhaps you're left-handed and have been given a workbook with the spiral binding on the left side. If any of these or similar situations have confronted you, then you know how common it is for individuals to struggle to adapt to their immediate environment or make use of a product. These issues are directly addressed by the principles of universal design, which is dedicated to creating buildings, products, and means of communication that are adjusted to users. Universal design provides the highest degree of usability to the greatest number of people in the most socially integrated setting possible. Its core concepts are an outgrowth of accessibility requirements developed years ago as people with disabilities gained their civil rights.

During the 1960s and 1970s, a growing national movement by members of the disability community drew attention to the belief that disabilities should not bar any individual from participating equally in society. They argued that it was not their physical conditions, but the design of the built environment, that created problems. Paraplegia, for example, didn't make a facility inaccessible, but rather the steps at its entrance did. Being deaf didn't jeopardize safety; the absence of visual alarms did.

The Rehabilitation Act of 1973 is recognized as the first U.S. law protecting the rights of people with all types of disabilities. Section 504 of this act mandated accessibility for all federally funded programs, services, and activities. New buildings and alterations of existing facilities covered under this act were to follow federal accessibility design guidelines. Facilities not undergoing alterations also had to provide accessibility, either through structural or non-structural changes, such as relocating an activity from an inaccessible room to an accessible one. The regulations refer to this as program accessibility. Public schools, which generally receive federal funds from a variety of sources, are therefore subject to the requirements of Section 504.

In 1990, the Americans with Disabilities Act (ADA) prohibited discrimination based on disability in employment, public accommodations, and state and local governments, including public school districts. The ADA Accessibility Guidelines (ADAAG) established minimum standards, but ADA's program accessibility regulations meant that states or local governments may sometimes need to go beyond those minimums in order to serve all their users.

Unfortunately, disability rights laws have not often been upheld. Many school districts have never implemented provisions for accessibility. Others misinterpreted program accessibility to mean simply the creation of an accessible entrance or the provision of an accessible toilet room on the first floor, and ignored the issue of vertical accessibility between floors. Many schools built prior to 1990 often have essential rooms like the gymnasium, library, or science and computer labs on upper floors that are inaccessible to students who cannot use stairs. Such an arrangement usually prevents a disabled student from receiving the "free, appropriate, public education" that the federal Individuals with Disabilities Education Act (IDEA) entitles him or her. This may likewise deny access to parents and members of the public who have disabilities.

One philosophical approach to making schools that serve people both with and without disabilities is universal design. This concept was pioneered in the 1970s by the late architect Ron Mace of the Center for Universal Design at North Carolina State University. While some individuals may argue that universal design is a different approach to design and architecture, it is in fact simply the application of good design practice to very diverse users. It does not change the design process, but expands it to address the needs of everyone. In the Chicago Public Schools Design Competition, universal design was one of the five fundamental criteria for judging. Elements in some of the winning designs demonstrate several of the seven commonly accepted principles of universal design.[1]

The first of these principles, *equitable use*, stipulates that the design is useful and marketable to people with diverse abilities, and that it provides the same means of use for all users – identical whenever possible, equivalent when not. Equitable use also avoids segregating or stigmatizing any user, and makes provisions for privacy, security, and safety equally available to all. Finally, it makes the design appealing to all users. Among the designs submitted for the competition, that of Borum, Daubmann, Hyde + Roddier incorporates the green features of exceptional thermal and acoustical insulation. Their interest may primarily reflect a desire to save energy and reduce costs, but such insulation also creates a better learning environment for students who have conditions exacerbated by temperature extremes. Students with hearing impairments, learning disabilities, or autism benefit from the noise attenuation.

The second principle, *flexibility in use*, ensures that a design accommodates a wide range of individual preferences and abilities. This may mean, for example, that it provides choice in methods of use, or accommodates left- or right-handed access and use. Attention to this principle facilitates the user's accuracy and precision and provides adaptability to the user's own pace. The Smith-Miller + Hawkinson submission includes a rendering of a classroom in which a student in a wheelchair is writing on a floor-to-ceiling chalkboard. The availability of a chalkboard appropriate for students and teachers of all heights is an appropriate instance of this principle.

The concept that design be *simple and intuitive* is the third principle of universal design. It calls for the use of design that is easy to understand, regardless of the user's experience, knowledge, language skills, or level of concentration. It asks that the designer eliminate unnecessary complexity and produce a design that is consistent with the user's expectations and intuition and accommodates a wide range of literacy and language skills. This principle is intended to ensure that information is provided to the user in a manner consistent with its importance and that a product, for example, provides effective prompting and feedback during and after use.

The fourth principle of universal design is *perceptible information*, by which is meant the effort to communicate necessary information effectively to the user, regardless of ambient conditions or the user's sensory abilities. This goal may involve the use of different modes (pictorial, verbal, tactile) for redundant presentation of essential information, the use of maximal legibility in the presentation of essential information, and the differentiation of elements in ways that can be described, thereby making it easy to give instructions or directions. Respect for this principle might also mean that a designer or architect creates in a way that is compatible with a variety of techniques or devices already used by people with sensory limitations. Thus, adherence to principles three and four would benefit people with sensory and cognitive disabilities, as well as individuals who are non-readers, those for whom English is not their first language, and those who have different cultural expectations than the majority population – all of which makes these principles very valuable in our increasingly diverse communities.

A *tolerance for errors* is the fifth principle of universal design – an approach that would minimize the hazards and adverse consequences of accidental or unintended actions. This principle would motivate designers to eliminate, isolate, or shield hazardous elements and keep the most used elements as the most accessible. It would ensure that they provide warnings of hazards and errors, build in fail-safe features, and discourage unconscious actions in tasks that require vigilance. A negative example of this principle can be observed in many "handi-capped" toilet rooms where the lavatories have blade hardware. Such hardware is not required by ADAAG and does not actually increase accessibility. It is, however, prone to breakage and vandalism that renders the lavatory unusable by everyone. Meanwhile, standard push-button hardware is accessible, durable, and cheaper.

The sixth principle asks that designers anticipate *low physical effort on the part of users*, creating a design that can be used efficiently and comfortably, with a minimum of fatigue. Adherence to this principle would allow the user to maintain a neutral body position and apply reasonable force to operate a device, while minimizing repetitive actions and sustained physical effort. Ramps, for example, even at a minimal degree of slope, challenge some people, particularly children who often lack the stamina and control to propel a wheel-chair on an incline. Individuals using crutches, canes, or walkers should not have to travel long distances, just as people who are blind or have low vision should not be required to travel indirect routes in unfamiliar settings. In recognition of this, the winning design by Koning Eizenberg depicts a parking area immediately adjacent to the school. Furthermore, public use areas, like the dining commons and multipurpose room, are located near the entrance, as is the elevator to the second-floor upper-grade "neighborhood," thereby minimizing travel distances for everyone.

Sometimes the absence of a typical building element can create accessibility. The prototype design for toilet rooms in the Chicago Public Schools, as exemplified in the drawings for this competition, omits doors at the entrances. Thoughtful layout allows all students to enter without the difficulty of maneuvering through entrance doors, while still maintaining privacy for restroom users.

Finally, the seventh principle addresses the concern that an *appropriate size and space are provided for approach, reach, manipulation, and use*, regardless of a user's body size, posture, or mobility. This issue requires designers to provide a clear line of sight to important elements whether the users are seated or standing. It also makes the reach to all components comfortable for seated or standing users and accommodates variations in hand and grip size. In addition, it ensures that design of the built environment provides adequate space for the use of assistive devices or personal assistance. In accordance with the ADAAG, a standard toilet room lavatory should be accessible for all children. Ironically, the elongated lavatory frequently marketed as appropriate for "the handicapped" is actually less accessible for many people, especially children, because the faucet controls at the back are beyond their reach. The elongated lavatory also violates the principle of providing the same means of use for all users.

Not Just a Good Idea, It's the Law

Many architects and designers recognized the need for accessibility and universal design long ago. Now that the ADA brings with it legal requirements, design professionals put public sector clients at risk if they fail to address accessibility and usability in an appropriate way. During the last decade, school districts across the country have been subjects of complaints to the U. S. Department of Education Office for Civil Rights or defendants in federal ADA compliance lawsuits. When found in violation of the ADA, districts have been compelled to create the accessibility they should have undertaken already, but now with the added burden of plaintiffs' attorneys' fees in addition to their own, as well as budgets and schedules determined by others.

These days, schools do much more than house pre-kindergarten through twelfth-grade classes. They are community centers hosting programs from infant day care to parent computer training. Many also serve as polling places. An inaccessible school, therefore, violates not only the rights of disabled students, but also those of disabled adults, whose taxes support the schools. Students with and without disabilities benefit educationally and socially from an integrated education that can only occur in an accessible facility. When they can freely interact as children, all students are better prepared for the workplace and civil society they will experience as adults. Now more than ever, school architects and design professionals should undergird their philosophy and designs with the principles of accessibility and universal design, giving all students their best chance for a great future.

1 The seven principles of universal design were compiled by Bettye Rose Connell, Mike Jones, Ron Mace, Jim Mueller, Abir Mullick, Elaine Ostroff, Jon Sanford, Ed Steinfeld, Molly Story, and Gregg Vanderheiden.

Sustainable School Building: Appreciation, Awareness, and Action

Thomas A. Forman, President
Chicago Associates Planners and Architects

Rose Grayson, Associate
Chicago Associates Planners and Architects

In spite of the increasing attention paid to sustainable building practices, the national and international movements championing the principles of sustainability face the difficult challenge of the public's uncertainty about its meaning and scope. While some individuals may think that sustainable design simply denotes an interest in energy efficiency, others may believe that it focuses primarily on the use of natural, or even alternative, building materials. Still others may associate its efforts with managing the bottom line. Regardless of these differences, however, a certain amount of confusion is justifiable, for sustainable building in fact includes all of these aspects. The term sustainability was first broadly defined in 1987 by the United Nations World Commission on Environment and Development in its report *Our Common Future*: "Sustainable development is development that meets the needs of the present without compromising the ability of future generations to meet their own needs."[1] Just as the World Commission on Environment and Development took up a wide range of issues related to economy and ecology – population, food, species diversity, energy, human settlements, and more – so too the cause of sustainable building will be best served by a broad-based approach. With the coordinated efforts of understanding and employing a host of new building materials and innovative technologies, we can reap the rewards of a healthier environment and improved indoor air quality. We can also enjoy the benefit of less negative impact on the environment, as sustainable buildings are, by their nature, more efficient – both environmentally and economically. In turn, many of these aspects of sustainable building will yield a further, positive effect on community sustainability.

The design of community-based learning environments – such as have been proposed by the Chicago Public Schools Design Competition – can significantly shape students' understanding of the world around them. They can foster an environmental ethic that will help students care for the land they will eventually inherit. As we begin to educate our children on the environment and the effect of our actions on it, they will become more sensitive to the manner in which they live. We can teach these lessons best through example. If we give children a healthy place in which to learn, with environmental strategies incorporated into their curriculum and built into the very fabric of the building that houses them, they will not only experience greater productivity but will also grow an increased awareness and appreciation for their immediate environment and their community at large. If we can emphasize that the school is the tangible precedent for children to learn sustainable practices, they will bring those efforts to their homes, encourage their families and communities, and continue the ongoing loop of sustainable living.

Over the last decade, many Americans have become increasingly aware of and sensitive to the significance of sustainability in their everyday lives. Nonetheless, sustainability is to some degree still considered unconventional, alternative, expensive, or exceptional. The efforts that are currently acknowledged and rewarded for sustainable design should become standard and routine in the design of our schools and other buildings – whether public, residential, or commercial. Sustainable design must, in short, become the model for all buildings. It must become the building strategy *expected* by clients. Nowhere can this vital message be taught more clearly and with greater impact than in our schools. Those who will learn its lessons, take them to heart, and carry them home are our children.

Schools designed according to the principles of sustainability are the best teachers of ecology. They communicate the power and potentials of ecological design and environmentally and socially responsible construction. These potentials can be seen through four lenses of sustainability: *partnership, enterprise, conservation,* and *design*. Each of these is interrelated, and the sustainable design of schools teaches us to understand these lenses. We understand their links and impacts on each other. Furthermore, we can evaluate the economic, ecological, physical, and social choices to make our neighborhoods more sustainable. These four lenses offer a variety of program and design orientations for the sustainable school building.

The first of these, *partnership,* implies social equity in building harmony within the school's diverse community. This inclusive process can bring all the people in the school together, bridging differences and promoting equality. The cost benefit of sustainability is understood through the second of these lenses, *enterprise* – in both the local and global economy. True cost accounting takes into consideration both short-term and long-term costs. "It is reported that the creation of buildings generates nearly 40 percent of United States landfill, consumes 25 percent of all harvested wood, and uses 3 billion tons of raw materials annually. Daily operation of these buildings (air conditioning, lighting, and powering electrical equipment) accounts for more than 30 percent of the total energy consumed in the United States and two-thirds of the electricity produced here."[2] The development of energy-efficient building, both from the point of view of operations and resource consumption, can promote the sustainable school.

The third lens, *conservation*, addresses the physical and natural environment concerns, seeking to preserve cultural diversity and skills, as well as the physical environment, locally and globally. This includes the natural environment, natural resources, rural land, and the urban and rural built environment. Finally, *design* is the concrete expression of the physical context in which the other three concerns can flourish. School buildings have evolved from the symbolic to the standardized, but they still have the potential to carry the message of sustainability to the community.

All of the submissions to the Chicago Public Schools Design Competition presented the judges the opportunity to evaluate the architects' commitment to sustainability. Each of the winning, finalist, and notable projects included in this book can also be examined through these four lenses to determine which aspects of sustainability have been considered. The following topics are some examples to look for as one evaluates the individual school designs.

Partnership

Learning from the sustainable school has been demonstrated in the "greening of the campus" movement across the country. Guidelines and programs have been designed so that learning becomes localized, tied to the cultures and communities of the bioregion, creating responsible citizens and focusing on interdisciplinary knowledge. Topics here could include energy conservation, environmentally sound procurement, environmentally sound ground maintenance, water prevention and recycling, green design, sustainable transportation, food production and the environment, water conservation, pollution prevention, healthy building, indoor air quality, and materials and resources. A variety of individual and collective projects can be developed within these topics – projects that would reflect the wide interests of the students, teachers, parents, and neighbors.

Learning from the sustainable school can be seen in what aspects have been utilized and how the students, teachers, parents, and residents engage in ongoing activities. The energy efficient school will create a better learning, teaching, and social environment; decrease the impact of the school on the environment; and lower its overall operating costs. Architects need to design the building shell to address radiant energy flows as well as conductive heat gain and loss, and select the optimum glazing configuration and window treatments for each location to maximize winter solar gain and minimize summer overheating. They can now consider a range of solar technologies, including daylighting, passive heating, domestic hot water and space heating, absorption cooling, building integrated photovoltaics, and exterior photovoltaic lighting systems, and they can manage the cost of solar systems by integrating them into overall design components. Daylighting, for example, can be incorporated into all teaching and learning spaces, and buildings can be oriented to maximize southern exposure and minimize east-west walls. In addition, designers can specify energy-efficient lighting systems that are compatible with the daylighting strategy and use full-spectrum lighting in well utilized, non-daylight spaces. They can utilize controls that reduce lighting levels in stages according to the amount of natural daylight in each space and linking these controls to other environmental systems. Mechanical and ventilation systems can also become more energy efficient and utilize waste heat wherever possible. They can improve indoor air quality by considering physical, biological, and chemical sources of potentially harmful contaminants and selecting environmentally friendly alternatives, and by using natural ventilation. The water conservation efforts of a sustainable school can involve harvesting rainwater from all surfaces of the building and its site for irrigation, toilet flushing, and water gardens. Architects and landscape architects together can avoid unnecessary water waste and consumption by incorporating low-flow and water conserving fixtures and native plants. In efforts that take a broader approach toward sustainable building, architects and project supervisors can specifying products that are made from recycled materials, that are locally produced, and that either do not pollute or have a low impact on operations. Finally, we can encourage contractors to recycle waste materials during construction, and provide elements to ease recycling by students, staff, parents, and neighbors.

The sustainable school can also present the entire community many opportunities for learning if the school site has been deliberately designed as a habitat for learning, with its physical realm serving as a setting for community sustainable programs, perhaps featuring a natural landscape, community gardens, soil revitalization, natural technologies for storm, gray, and waste water renewal, and a sustainable transportation connection to the neighborhood. The school site will take place in the web of nature by integrating community activities and natural technologies. The natural landscape can be organized into a pattern of ecological spaces that have the potential for providing social and economic benefits. These ecological spaces can become ideal habitats for gardens and nurseries for plants that thrive in the urban environment. They can also be served by a water infrastructure that provides for on-site treatment, retention, and distribution of storm, gray, and waste waters. These functions in turn can be forged into urban enterprise involving students, teachers, parents, and neighbors. The site can also become a source for energy resource self-sufficiency with windmill fields and geothermal cells to generate energy for the school that may potentially be shared with its neighbors as well. Finally, the learning habitat – appropriately designed with native plant species – will become a haven for wildlife: birds, mammals, insects, and fish will find refuge on the school site.

Design

Learning from the sustainable school is possible if we focus on the classroom as a setting for a healthy and productive learning community. The sustainable school can feature natural daylight and ventilation; a comfortable acoustical, thermal, and visual environment; and a year-round connection between the inside and outside – all while maintaining air quality, safety, and security. Windows can be placed in the façade to provide daylight throughout the school, controlling sunlight and providing a view to the outdoor learning habitat. Students, teachers, parents, and neighbors will become aware of how sunlight provides a changing texture and quality of light, and assists in creating an acoustically and visually comfortable classroom as it is brought into the space through windows, clerestories, and skylights. The value of natural ventilation can be provided in a variety of ways: operative windows, vented walls, and sensor-operated transoms. In all cases, the daylight and ventilation will be introduced into the classroom in order to assure a safe and secure environment for learning. Similarly, all materials used in the classroom will be healthy and resource efficient. Furthermore, the resource and material management will contribute to the health of the planet.

  In conclusion, one of the potentials of the sustainable school is the ability to measure the impacts of the different improvement programs, which can be selected to test and communicate a variety of methods, systems, and materials. Additionally, these measurements should meet the following criteria: appropriateness to the scope of work of the school building; and comprehensiveness, from general to specific, so that the classroom impacts the school, the school impacts the community.

Gradually, educators, designers, civic leaders, and citizens are beginning to care about sustainable design. They are recognizing the necessity for livable environments that will not only help to sustain the earth, but also aid in sustaining the well-being of those interacting within a microenvironment. What have we done by making buildings that are fast, cheap, and easy to reproduce and replace? The building materials are toxic, the air isn't clean, and both the buildings and their users fall sick from these unnatural environments! If we can harness the benefits of environmental sustainability for use in both our community and local economy, the rewards will soon be apparent at global levels as well. If we use our schools as the host to carry out this plan, then we will surely see the results. Schools are places of learning for children and adults alike. Beyond their function as classrooms for several hours a day, they are community meeting places for education and recreation and civic centers for resources and the exchange of information. We must now focus on developing these core educational spaces as places where entire communities can learn the importance and effects of sustainable practices.

1 World Commission on Environment and Development, *Our Common Future* (New York: Oxford University Press, 1987).

2 D. Roodman and N. Lensaen, *A Building Revolution: How Ecology and Health Concerns Are Transforming Construction,* Worldwatch Paper no. 124 (Washington, D. C.: Worldwatch Institute, 1995), p. 22.

Trends in School
Design and Construction

Jeffery A. Lackney, Ph.D., AIA, REFP
University of Wisconsin-Madison

National expenditure for school construction in the year 2000 was the largest in United States history. Over $21 billion was spent on schools, with nearly half of this amount earmarked for over 700 new school buildings.[1] The first two years of the twenty-first century have produced similar results, in keeping with an upward trend in spending on new school construction that continued throughout the 1990s. In 1995, for instance, a record $10.3 billion was expended, and the growth in spending culminated in school construction totals in the year 2000 that exceeded actual school construction expenditures in 1974 – a year that represented the peak of spending during the postwar baby boom.[2]

If we are to come close to meeting our enormous (and increasing) national need in this area, continued educational and governmental leadership will be vital. Without such leadership it will be difficult to maintain throughout the United States the record school construction spending trends that have been established in recent years. Estimates of the cost to repair and modernize school facilities nationwide were cited in the 1989 Education Writers Association study at $41 billion.[3] That figure climbed to $112 billion as estimated by the U.S. General Accounting Office (GAO) in its landmark 1995 report.[4] The National Center for Education Statistics (NCES) estimated a national need of $127 billion in 1999,[5] and within a year that total was put at $322 billion by the National Education Association.[6] The NCES study, echoing reports by the GAO, estimated that over three-fourths of all U.S. schools – or approximately 59,400 school buildings – needed to expend on average more than $2 million per school building to effect repairs and complete renovations or modernizations simply to get their schools in overall good condition. Indeed, even by spending at a record pace of over $20 billion per year, it may take another full decade or more before school facility needs are adequately met. The U.S. Congress continues to introduce bills for school construction, and the latest of these, America's Better Classroom Act of 2001, would make $25.2 billion in funds available through the use of tax-credit bonds.

Along with this new, unprecedented era of school construction comes the challenge to implement well-reasoned principles of school design that respond proactively to changes in education, rather than simply replicating existing school buildings that perhaps accommodated an educational philosophy tailored to an earlier, industrially based society. Although educational reforms are diverse, there appears to be agreement concerning the need for smaller schools and smaller classes that emphasize learner-centered, hands-on, project-oriented, experiential learning, personalized and interdisciplinary instruction, and a thematic and integrated curriculum. In addition, a growing emphasis on universal design has responded to calls that we recognize diversity and accessibility in school settings: schools are once again becoming true centers of our communities, and they can readily serve as places for life-long learning for more ethnically and age diverse community populations. Design principles that address such educational reforms have recently been set forth in an excellent publication by the U.S. Department of Education entitled *Design Principles for Designing Schools as Centers of Community*.[7]

Unfortunately, these design principles, or new trends in school design, are not being adhered to in school construction today as strictly as would be preferred. More than a handful of local communities, however, recognize that in addition to a school building being cost-effective, it should also be more learner-centered, developmentally appropriate, and age appropriate, as well as safe, comfortable, accessible, flexible, diverse, and equitable.

Can these design principles that most citizens hold as keys to improved twenty-first-century learning be accomplished with the same construction budgets as conventionally designed schools? The answer is an emphatic yes. Certainly they can. In fact, the 2001 Chicago Public Schools Design Competition, entitled "Big Shoulders, Small Schools," provides a clear answer that the cost of constructing schools for the twenty-first century is in no way different from the cost of constructing schools for the previous century.

One unique design criteria established in the CPS competition was a budget feasibility requirement limiting the cost of construction. Taking into consideration the unique urban site conditions established for this competition, a budget of $160 per square foot for construction cost was established.[8] This budget is equivalent to the highest quartile of national median costs for elementary and middle schools ($157.89 per square foot) in the U.S. for school construction ending in 2001.[9] Based on this comparison of construction cost, one could anticipate that the estimates for these design proposals would vary depending on the region of the country. There are, in fact, a wide range of well-known factors that can affect the actual construction cost of any school building: site location, whether rural, suburban, or urban; unique site constraints; weather conditions; time of year; local labor laws; and the state of the economy.

What the Chicago Public Schools Design Competition illustrates is not only a new way of thinking about school facilities as an active contributor to the educational process, but also a new willingness finally to act on what has been learned from decades of research on small schools, universal design, and class size. Over a brief span of time, architects and educators have collaborated to implement a positive change in the school environment. It is, inarguably, time to make these new trends the norm.

These new trends will not become the norm, however, unless they can demonstrate cost-effectiveness. A number of recent trends, such as increasing community involvement and creating community-centered schools, emphasizing safe and secure school design, planning for information technology, and designing high-performance building systems, all lead the way in meeting the dual goals of providing a cost-effective and learner-centered school.

Evidence of this movement is already apparent. School leaders and planners have begun to involve a much wider spectrum of the community during the planning and design of schools than in the past, inviting parents, business and community leaders, teachers, and, in a few cases, students to take part in the process. School leaders have discovered that by doing so they can avoid many public relations roadblocks and settle upon school designs that are cost-effective and responsive to the specific needs of the taxpaying community.

The natural outgrowth of wider *community participation* has been the gradual trans-formation of the traditional school building into a center for community learning. By locating new school facilities in residential neighborhoods and networking the school with other community-based organizations, schools are becoming true *community centers*, serving broader societal goals and providing settings for meaningful civic participation and engagement. Sharing community resources through partnerships with theatres, museums, libraries, commu-nity centers, government and community organizations, and private sector businesses has become a well-traveled path for effectively extending the financial resources available to a school without committing additional dollars for expensive redundant facilities.

We have known for some time that in comparison to the large schools of thousands of students, *small schools* can offer students greater opportunities to exercise leadership and to participate in school activities.[10] Student satisfaction, number of classes taken, community employment, and participation in social organizations have all been found to be greater in small schools. Meanwhile, incidents of crime and student misconduct correspondingly decrease in small schools. This research invites action. School leaders and school designers have seriously begun to make the move toward building smaller schools – at all levels of education. Along with the trend toward creating smaller schools inside existing larger ones (i.e., schools-within-schools), a related approach of decreasing the physical scale of many school buildings is also taking place.

The design of *safe schools* increasingly recognizes the desirability of providing natural, unobtrusive surveillance rather than installing checkpoints and security guards that ultimately add to both the initial capital expenditure and the long-term operating costs. The recognition that our schools should not have the look and feel of prisons has led many school leaders to consider other approaches to building design that, in concert with various violence-prevention programs, reduce both the fear of crime and the incidence of crime. Small schools allow for both natural surveillance and territorial ownership: students and teachers are on familiar terms, thereby decreasing the possibility that any one student is overlooked socially or psychologically.[11]

The self-contained classroom can no longer provide the variety of learning settings that are necessary to support authentic, project-based, real-world learning and methods of assessment. Smaller class sizes are now an accepted factor contributing in some measure to *improved achievement*. The increased costs of constructing additional classrooms and hiring more teachers cannot be overlooked, but neither can the social and psychological costs of failing to decrease average class size.

Recent developments in information technology have precipitated a variety of changes in the organizational and physical form of our schools and have brought with it an added expense that was not present only a decade ago. With respect to instructional processes, *information technology* is rapidly facilitating the movement toward self-directed learning and individualized instruction. But even as learning becomes increasingly virtual and Web-based, it still must occur somewhere physically. At present, information technology is often unevenly distributed in isolated computer labs in schools, with perhaps a few computers scattered around the school building in instructional areas and media centers. As information technology becomes ubiquitous, more schools will decentralize access to it, distributing it throughout the school building and across the community. The impact of this trend on schools is yet uncertain, but one clear result is that more and more formal learning will take place outside the school building, freeing space within the school building for other educational purposes and programs and allowing for a natural reduction in class size without the cost of new classrooms. According to some critics, it is entirely possible that the need for additional instructional space will slow, actually decreasing the cost for constructing new facilities in the future.

The trend toward *smart or high-performance buildings* (i.e., buildings that are designed and constructed to integrate the technologies of instruction, telecommunications, and building systems) will have increased responsiveness to the needs of its occupants, as well as to the educational process. Smart buildings are being designed with a host of environmental and occupant sensors that can regulate natural light and artificial full-spectrum lighting, thereby minimizing mental fatigue and reducing hyperactivity, as well as provide better monitoring of indoor air quality, heating, ventilation, and air conditioning. Concern over the initial costs of these systems has proven unnecessary in many high-performance schools: energy efficiency savings are already offsetting initial investments.[12]

The potential payoff of our investment in school facilities, in social as well as economic terms, cannot be ignored in light of what we know about the impact that facilities exert on learning. Recognition and implementation of these innovative ideas among a growing number of school districts have begun to yield some clear trends in school design and construction that other school communities can follow confidently.

1 P. Abramson, "2001 Construction Report," *School Planning and Management* (February 2001), pp. 27–44.

2 Ibid.

3 Education Writers Association, *Wolves at the Schoolhouse Door: An Investigation of the Condition of Public School Buildings* (Washington, D.C.: Education Writers Association, 1989).

4 U.S. General Accounting Office, *School Facilities: Condition of America's Schools*, GAO/HEHS–95–61 (Washington, D.C.: U.S. General Accounting Office, 1995). See also U.S. General Accounting Office, *School Facilities: Construction Expenditures Have Grown Significantly in Recent Years*, GAO/HEHS–00–41 (Washington, D.C.: U.S. General Accounting Office, 2000).

5 Laurie Lewis, Kyle Snow, Elizabeth Farris, Becky Smerdon, Stephanie Cronen, Jessica Kaplan, and Bernie Greene, *Condition of America's Public School Facilities: 1999* (Washington, D.C.: National Center for Education Statistics, 2000).

6 National Education Association, *Modernizing Our Schools: What Will It Cost?* (Washington, D.C.: National Education Association, 2000).

7 See http://www.edfacilities.org/ir/edprinciples.html.

8 A budget figure for each school was set at $200 per square foot (in 2000 dollars), an amount that was to include soft costs and furniture, but not expenditures for land, utilities, remediation, or medical equipment. Soft costs were established at 20% of total costs, bringing the construction cost to $160 per square foot.

9 See Abramson (note 1), table 5, p. 32.

10 Mary Anne Raywid, *Current Literature on Small Schools*, EDO-RC-98-8 (Washington, D.C.: ERIC Clearinghouse on Rural Education and Small Schools, 1999).

11 Timothy D. Crowe, *Crime Prevention through Environmental Design: Applications of Architectural Design and Space Management Concepts* (Boston: Butterworth-Heinemann and National Crime Prevention Institute, 2000).

12 Sustainable Buildings Industry Council, *Resource and Strategy Guide: High Performance School Buildings* (Washington, D.C.: Sustainable Buildings Industry Council, 2001).

Acknowledgments

E. Hoy McConnell, II, Executive Director
Business and Professional People for the Public Interest

Cindy S. Moelis, Director, Education Initiative
Business and Professional People for the Public Interest

This publication represents a collaborative effort among many people in the fields of architecture, education, and public policy. Without their support and consultation, this book would not have been possible. We want to extend our deep appreciation to all who contributed their talent, wisdom, and energy to the Chicago Public Schools Design Competition, which produced the innovative school designs highlighted in this publication. We would also like to express our gratitude and lend our support to those working to get these schools built.

First, we thank our funders, who while extending generous financial support, also provided exceptional guidance and commitment. Richard Driehaus and Sunny Fischer of The Richard H. Driehaus Foundation were instrumental in inspiring and conceptualizing the competition process and helped extensively with the execution of the competition and this publication. David Logan of the Reva and David Logan Foundation provided critical funding to support this book and is offering financial incentives to encourage the Chicago Board of Education to build the schools. Former National Endowment for the Arts Director of Design Mark Robbins and Graham Foundation Executive Director Richard Solomon provided ongoing input and direction.

We extend special appreciation to the Board of Education of the Chicago Public Schools (CPS) and specifically to CEO Arne Duncan, President Michael Scott, and board members Norman Bobins, Dr. Tariq Butt, Avis LaVelle, Clare Muñana, Gene Saffold, and Chief of Staff Brandy Turco, as well as former CPS officials Gery Chico, Paul Vallas, Jean Franczyk, and Michael Mayo, for recognizing the need and resolving to build these innovative schools. The continuing commitment of CPS staff members Giacomo Mancuso, Tim Martin, and Jeanne Nowaczewski will prove to be instrumental in ensuring that these designs become a reality.

We also wish to thank the 250 parents and students who traveled to Springfield to meet with state legislators and dramatize the need for these new schools. Likewise, we applaud the leadership of Principals Rochelle Riddick, Dick Smith, Eva Helwing, and Earl Ware, and Assistant Principal Minnie Watson in this effort. Special thanks go to Marissa Hopkins for her boundless energy and efforts; her ultimate reward will be the new community schools benefiting the Irving Park and Roseland communities.

We want to acknowledge here the hard work, extraordinary vision, and creative energy of every architect who competed in this project. Architect Karen Fairbanks deserves special commendation for her assistance and continuing dedication to the schools. We hope that her vision of a community garden at the South Side site will blossom in the spring of 2003.

The tireless efforts of many more ensured that the competition was community-driven and professionally executed, and we are grateful to the individuals and organizations listed on the next two pages who made this happen—from the jury's experts, educators, and community representatives to the diverse representatives on the Steering Committee.

We also want to extend our appreciation to the institutions that aided in this production: The Art Institute of Chicago, Chicago Historical Society, and Chicago Public Schools Research Center.

A number of individuals, not previously acknowledged, played instrumental roles of varying kinds: Mary Anderson, Karen Bausman, Aisha Bunton, Alana Cherlin, Pamela Clarke, Al Corbett, Peter Cunningham, Jaime deLeon, Ellen Elias, Kate Friedman, Jesus Garcia, Julia Gilfillan, Karen Girolami Callam, Sharon Haar, Jessica Haber, Dianne Hanau-Strain, Paula Kruger, Keith McClinton, Zoe Mikva, Jeff Ollswang, Jon Randolph, Beatriz Rendon, Jane Saks, Belkis Santos, Karla Seelandt, Anna Siegler, Anka Twum-Baah, Beth Valukas, and Larry Witzling. We are especially grateful to former BPI staffers Jeanne Nowaczewski, Jamie Hendrickson, and Jennifer Salvatore, who devoted many evenings and weekends to the success of this endeavor at every stage.

We extend special thanks to studio blue for their superb graphic design work and to editor Robert Sharp for his patience and editorial acumen.

Finally, we are very grateful to our competition cosponsors – the Chicago Public Schools, Leadership for Quality Education, and the Mayor's Office for People with Disabilities – for their vision and commitment to this project and to the schoolchildren of Chicago.

Competition Jurors

William Ayers, University of Illinois at Chicago, College of Education
Lance Jay Brown, City College of the City University of New York,
    School of Architecture
Marissa Hopkins, Inter-American Magnet School
Ralph E. Johnson, Perkins & Will
M. David Lee, Stull & Lee, Incorporated
Giacomo Mancuso, Chicago Public Schools
Linda Owens, Davis Developmental Center
Brigitte Shim, Shim Sutcliffe Architects
Richard G. Smith, Frederick Stock School
Dennis Vail, Langston Hughes School

Competition Funders

The Richard H. Driehaus Foundation
Reva and David Logan Foundation

Graham Foundation for Advanced Studies in the Fine Arts
The Joyce Foundation
National Endowment for the Arts

Additional support provided by:
Chicago Architecture Foundation
Chicago Association of Realtors Education Foundation
George L. Jewell Catering Services, Inc.
Nuveen Investments
Oppenheimer Family Foundation
Polk Bros. Foundation
Prince Charitable Trusts
United Airlines

Winning, Finalist, and Notable Architects

Winner, North Side

Koning Eizenberg Architecture

Hendrik Koning, Julie Eizenberg, Jason Kerwin, Julio Zavolta

1454 25th Street

Santa Monica, California 90404

Tel.: 310-828-6131 x 112; fax: 310-828-0719

www.kearch.com

Winner, South Side

Marble Fairbanks Architects

Scott Marble, Karen Fairbanks

66 W. Broadway, #600

New York, New York 10007

Tel.: 212-233-0653; fax: 212-233-0654

www.marblefairbanks.com

Finalists, North Side

Jack L. Gordon Architects

Sophie Ladjimi, John Ingram, Jack Gordon

43 W. 23rd Street

New York, New York 10010

Tel.: 212-633-0909; fax: 212-633-2085

Lubrano Ciavarra Design

Lea Ciavarra, Anne Marie Lubrano, Richard Nisa

594 Broadway, Studio 404

New York, New York 10012

Tel.: 212-404-7575; fax: 212-404-7574

www.IcNYC.com

Ross Barney + Jankowski Architects
Carol Ross Barney, Laura Saviano
10 W. Hubbard Street
Chicago, Illinois 60610
Tel.: 312-832-0600; fax: 312-832-0601

Finalists, South Side

Borum, Daubmann, Hyde + Roddier
Craig Borum, Karl Daubmann, Olivia Hyde, Mireille Roddier,
John Comazzi, Kristen Dean, Carl Lorenz, Loren Meyer, Bryon Murdock,
Gretchen Wilkins, Maurya McClintock (Ove Arup+Partners), Jelena
Srebric, Kevin Benham, Jerrod Kowalewski
308-1/2 S. State Street, Suite 30
Ann Arbor, Michigan 48104
Tel.: 734-827-2238; fax: 734-994-3328

Mack Scogin Merrill Elam Architects
Merrill Elam, Mack Scogin, Christopher Agosta, Brian Bell,
Tim Harrison, Barum Tiller, Ted Paxton, Charlotte Henderson, Penn
Ruderman, Dustin Lindblad
75 John Wesley Dobbs Avenue, N.E.
Atlanta, Georgia 30303
Tel.: 404-525-6869; fax: 404-525-7061

Smith-Miller + Hawkinson Architects
Henry Smith-Miller, Laurie Hawkinson, Starling Keene
305 Canal Street
New York, New York 10013
Tel.: 212-966-3875; fax: 212-966-3877

Notable Architects

Garofalo Architects, Inc.
Douglas Garofalo AIA
3752 N. Ashland Avenue
Chicago, Illinois 60613
Tel.: 773-975-2069; fax: 773-975-3005
www.garofalo.a-node.net

CODA Group (Content Design Architecture)
Sze Tsung Leong, Chuihua Judy Chung, Ho-San Chung
49 Bleeker Street, Suite 303
New York, New York 10012
Tel.: 212-228-1030; fax: 212-228-1174
mail@codagroup.net

Valerio Dewalt Train Associates, Inc.
Susanna Craib-Cox
500 N. Dearborn Street, 9th Floor
Chicago, Illinois 60610
Tel.: 312-332-0363; fax: 312-332-4727

Funkehavs Design
Jeffrey Funke
514 N. Noble
Chicago, Illinois 60622
Tel.: 312-919-1349; fax: 312-896-1200
JeffreyFunke@hotmail.com

Rogers Marvel Architects PLLC
Robert M. Rogers, principal; Jonathan Jova Marvel, principal
145 Hudson Street, 3rd Floor
New York, New York 10013
Tel.: 212-941-6718; fax: 212-941-7573
www.rogersmarvel.com

Urban Instruments, Inc.
Patti Reiter, Duke Reiter
424 Newtonville Avenue
Newton, Massachusetts 02460
Tel.: 617-559-0502; fax: 617-965-0289

Gonzalez Hasbrouck

Joe Gonzalez
180 N. Wabash Avenue
Chicago, Illinois 60601
Tel.: 312-458-1200; fax: 312-458-1202

Griffin Enright Architects

Margaret Griffin, John A. Enright
12468 Washington Blvd
Los Angeles, California 90066
Tel.: 310-391-4484; fax: 310-391-4495
www.griffinenrightarchitects.com

STL Architects

Susan Conger-Austin, Jose Luis De La Fuente
401 N. Wabash Avenue, Suite 623
Chicago, Illinois 60611
Tel.: 312-644-9850; fax: 312-644-9846

Frederic Schwartz Architects

180 Varick Street, 15th Floor
New York, New York 10014
Tel.: 212-741-3021; fax: 212-741-2346

von Weise Architects

Brian Vitale
417 S. Dearborn Street, Suite 800
Chicago, Illinois 60605
Tel.: 312-341-1155; fax: 312-341-1177
www.vwachicago.com

Educational Partners
and Resources

21st Century School Fund
Mary Filardo, Executive Director
2814 Adams Mill Road, NW
Washington, D.C. 20009
www.csf.org

Access Living
Marca Bristo, President and CEO
614 W. Roosevelt Road
Chicago, Illinois 60607

ADA Compliance Consultant
Shelley Sandow
115 Marengo, #508
Forest Park, Illinois 60130

Business and Professional People
for the Public Interest
Cindy Moelis, Director,
Education Initiative
25 E. Washington, Suite 1515
Chicago, Illinois 60602
www.bpichicago.org

Center for City Schools
National Louis University
122 S. Michigan Avenue, Suite 5044
Chicago, Illinois 60603
www.nl.edu

Chicago Associates Planners and
Architects
Thomas A. Forman, President
1840 W. Sunnyside
Chicago, Illinois 60640

Chicago Public Schools
Office of Small Schools
Jeanne L. Nowaczewski, Director
125 S. Clark Street
Chicago, Illinois 60603
www.cps.k12.il.us

Design Competition Services, Inc.
Jeff Ollswang
616 E. Lakeview Drive
Milwaukee, Wisconsin 53217

LCM Architects, LLC
John H. (Jack) Catlin, AIA
819 S. Wabash Avenue
Chicago, Illinois 60605

Leadership for Quality Education
John Ayers, Executive Director
One Bank One Plaza
21 S. Clark Street, Suite 3120
Chicago, Illinois 60603
www.lqe.org

Mayor's Office for People
with Disabilities
David K. Hanson, Commissioner
121 N. LaSalle Street, Room 1104
Chicago, Illinois 60602
http://www.ci.chi.il.us/Disabilities/

National Clearinghouse
for Education Facilities
1090 Vermont Avenue, NW, Suite 700
Washington, D.C. 20005
www.edfacilities.org

Neighborhood Capital Budget Group
Andrea Lee
407 S. Dearborn, Suite 1360
Chicago, IL 60605
www.ncbg.org

New Jersey Institute of Technology
Leslie Weisman, Professor of
Architecture
University Heights
Newark, New Jersey 07102-1982
www.njit.edu

Small Schools Workshop
Michael Klonsky, Director
Susan Klonsky, Director of Development
University of Illinois at Chicago
1640 W. Roosevelt Road, 6th Floor
Chicago, Illinois 60607
www.smallschoolsworkshop.org

University of Illinois at Chicago,
College of Education
William Ayers, Distinguished Professor
of Education
1040 W. Harrison Street, Room 3404
Chicago, Illinois 60607

University of Illinois at Chicago,
School of Architecture
Sharon Haar, Assistant Professor
845 W. Harrison Street
Room 3100 (m/c 030)
Chicago, Illinois 60607-7024

University of Wisconsin-Madison,
Department of Engineering
Jeffery A. Lackney, Assistant Professor
432 N. Lake Street, Room 825B
Madison, Wisconsin 53706-1498